Our Global Village
Second Edition

Our Global Village
Second Edition

Angela Labarca
Georgia Institute of Technology

James M. Hendrickson

Harcourt Brace College Publishers

Fort Worth   Philadelphia   San Diego   New York   Orlando   Austin   San Antonio
Toronto   Montreal   London   Sydney   Tokyo

Publisher Christopher Carson
Market Strategist Kenneth S. Kasee
Developmental Editors Pam Hatley; Mary Mayo
Project Editor Jon Davies
Art Director Garry Harman
Production Manager James McDonald

Cover credit: Sandra Dionisi The Stock Illustration Source

ISBN: 0-03-022256-7
Library of Congress Catalog Card Number: 98-87493

Address for Orders
Holt, Rinehart and Winston, 6277 Sea Harbor Drive, Orlando, FL 32887-6777
1-800-782-4479

Address for Editorial Correspondence
Holt, Rinehart and Winston, 301 Commerce Street, Suite 3700, Fort Worth, TX 76102

Web Site Address
http://www.hbcollege.com

Printed in the United States of America

9 0 1 2 3 4 5 6 7 8   039   9 8 7 6 5 4 3 2

Holt, Rinehart and Winston
Harcourt Brace College Publishers

The authors dedicate
Our Global Village
Second Edition

to the memory of Sharon Hendrickson
and to all teachers of English as a second or foreign
language as they begin educating their students for an
exciting new millennium.

Preface

Our Global Village is an intermediate-level reader designed for students of English as a second or foreign language. The book can also be used by native English-speakers enrolled in developmental and remedial reading programs offered by high schools, colleges, universities, and other educational institutions. Its primary purpose is to aid students in acquiring English through active participation in a variety of learning activities. A broader goal of the book is to help students learn some formal aspects of English, increase their vocabulary knowledge, and further develop their oral and written proficiency in English.

As its title indicates, this book has a strong cross-cultural focus. The authors have included reading selections on a broad range of human interest themes and geographical regions of the world. These readings, together with the learning activities, are intended to help students enjoy improving their English-language skills and become more acquainted with their classmates and the world community.

Acknowledgments

The authors wish to thank the following people for their contribution in producing this second edition of *Our Global Village:* Susan Marshall for serving as our acquisitions editor; Pam Hatley and Mary Mayo for managing the editorial process of the project; and James McDonald for supervising the book's production. We are also very grateful to the many thousands of students and instructors who enjoyed using the first edition of *Our Global Village.*

Angela Labarca
James M. Hendrickson

To the Instructor

Our Global Village contains fourteen chapters and seven vocabulary reviews. Each chapter is divided into three sections: a reading selection, learning activities, and a chapter vocabulary.

Reading Selections. Thirteen reading selections in this book are adaptations of articles that appeared in different English-language magazines; one reading selection is based on a coauthor's personal experience. The authors chose these articles primarily for their high student interest and for their wide range of geographic locations—from teaching infants to swim at children's centers in Russia and rescuing baby elephants in Kenya to a chat with the King of Tonga and discovering extraterrestrial sightings in Mexico. As these examples indicate, the readings consist of a collection of interesting slices of life from different regions of our interdependent world community—our "global village."

The primary function of these reading selections is the improvement of basic reading skills through enjoyable reading material in English. A broader goal of the readings is to facilitate students' progress in reading English-language materials in their adapted form. Some complex grammatical structures were replaced with shorter, simpler sentences, and some terms or expressions were either replaced with simpler ones or accompanied by a gloss note in the margin. Other lexical or topical items that required clarification are explained in footnotes.

The reading selections are sequenced in order of difficulty from the beginning of the book to the end. Essentially, the sequence of the readings was based on their readability as measured by the following four instruments:

1. *Flesch Reading Ease:* Computes readability based on the average number of syllables per word and the average number of words per sentence. Scores range from 0 (zero) to 100. Standard writing averages approximately 60 to 70. The higher the score, the greater the number of people who can easily understand the text.
2. *Flesch-Kincaid Grade Level:* Computes readability based on the average number of syllables per word and the average number of words per sentence. The score in this case indicates a grade-school level. For example, a score of 8.0 means that an eighth grader would understand the document. Standard writing equates approximately to the seventh-to-eighth-grade level.

3. *Coleman-Liau Grade Level:* Uses word length in characters and sentence length to determine a grade level.
4. *Bormuth Grade Level:* Uses word length in characters and sentence length in words to determine a grade level.

The authors made additional modifications in the sequence of the readings, within a narrow readability range, according to seven themes: Children and Animals, Family Ties, Foreign Travel, Home Entertainment, Human Life Sciences, Business Affairs, and The Future.

Learning Activities. The learning activities in *Our Global Village* provide many opportunities for students to improve their proficiency in reading and using English to express themselves in conversation and in writing. The majority of the learning activities are open-ended—that is, they do not require specific responses from students. In some of the activities a question mark prompts students to give other appropriate answers apart from those provided. Answers to all the close-ended activities appear in the Answer Key at the end of the book.

The kinds of learning activities vary considerably from chapter to chapter. They accommodate differences in learning strategies, topic interests, and depth of analysis. The activities include reading comprehension, reading strategies, pronunciation, vocabulary building, grammar practice, small-group discussions, writing tasks, and independent study projects.

Reading Comprehension. Reading comprehension exercises check a student's understanding of the reading selections. Varied formats are used to evaluate how well students have understood what they read and to help them develop efficient analytic skills. The formats include answering questions, true-false statements, multiple choice questions, compiling brief lists, rank ordering events, matching columns of information, and completing charts.

Reading Strategies. Many learning activities in the book provide practice in extracting information from the reading selections. Students are directed to scan paragraphs for main ideas, to infer meaning with the assistance of contextual clues, and to organize information into meaningful chunks for easier recall by using charts, graphs, and tables. These kinds of activities develop students' confidence in reading unfamiliar materials in English by using some strategies applied unconsciously in their first language. Such structured activities encourage students to become more independent readers.

Pronunciation. Significant features of spoken English appear in several chapters. Pronunciation exercises drill individual sounds, linking, and intonation patterns.

Vocabulary Building. These exercises appear in many different formats throughout the book. For example, students use idiomatic and figurative language, analyze word families and word sets, complete crossword puzzles, match associated words and phrases, and use synonyms and antonyms.

Grammar Practice. Students complete varied exercises for understanding the functions of different morphological elements and syntactic structures of English. These exercises are always presented in the context of a chapter's theme. They include, for example, practice in using third person present tense -*s*, in completing regular and irregular past tense verb forms, in using regular and irregular comparative adjectives, and in making comparisons.

Small-Group Discussions. An abundant variety of activities invites students to share their thoughts and feelings with their classmates in response to what they have read in the reading selections. Most of these activities are cross-culturally oriented; that is, students compare and contrast information based on their own social and cultural backgrounds. In this way students develop a better understanding and appreciation of our world community as well as a greater insight into ideas that differ from their own. Small-group activities include interviews, role playing, free interaction through problem solving, surveys, group consensus activities, debates, and various small-group projects.

Writing Tasks. The book includes activities for expanding communication in writing. Students are given specific writing tasks such as expressing opinions, narrating an event, and taking notes. Students can subsequently incorporate the text produced into other pieces such as letters.

Independent Study Projects. These projects encourage students to investigate in depth specific topics introduced in the reading selections and in some of the other learning activities. Students are asked to report their findings either orally or in writing. By seeking, discovering, and reporting information in this way, students not only improve their ability to communicate effectively in English but also expand their knowledge of our world community and their own unique place in it.

Chapter Vocabularies. Every chapter ends with a list of content words and phrases that appear in its reading selection. The vocabulary lists are divided into categories of nouns, adjectives, verbs, adverbs, proper nouns, and expressions. Each word or expression is listed alphabetically within its respective category.

The vocabulary lists are a useful tool for students and their instructors. The lists provide a reference for reviewing lexical items for testing. They also serve as a resource for grouping words into thematic or functional categories (e.g., *family, mother, father*), for understanding and using words appropriately (e.g., *earth, land, ground*), for studying morphological features (e.g., *beautiful, wonderful, grateful*), and for recognizing and using synonyms and antonyms. The authors encourage instructors to experiment with these and other reading strategies for helping their students become more proficient and independent learners of English.

The Vocabulary Reviews. The seven vocabulary reviews, one after every thematic unit, contain activities for using common words and phrases that appear in the reading selections. These reviews present five different kinds of activities. **Word sets** are exercises that help students associate words in semantic categories. **Reading for meaning** activities are word replacement exercises that focus on a topic presented in one of the two readings on which a given vocabulary review is based. **Which do you prefer?** activities provide students with opportunities to express their likes, dislikes, and opinions about many topics. **Getting to know you** are interview activities that encourage students to become better acquainted with their classmates. **Crossword puzzles** are entertaining exercises based on word definitions.

Contents

Our Global Village

Second Edition

UNIT I

CHILDREN
AND
ANIMALS

1 | Swim First, Walk Later

Before babies walk, many of them learn how to swim at children's centers. There are centers for children in the United States, Japan, Austria, Germany, England, and Russia. The slogan° in these centers is "Swim first, walk later."

important phrase

Igor Charkovsky is a swimming instructor in Russia. He says that teaching babies to swim is easy. "First, lower the baby to the water. Wait for the moment when the baby begins to exhale.° Then gently submerge° the baby into the water. Babies float up to the surface° easily. Teach the infants° to hold their breath° for two seconds, then for a longer period. Babies learn very fast."

breathe out
put / top
babies / not breathe

In Moscow many infants swim in pools at special polyclinics.° They are stronger and healthier than babies who do not swim. Also, they are happy, relaxed, and not afraid of water. These babies are happy because they enjoy themselves so much in the swimming pool, instead of crying in their cradles.° They are also very healthy; on the average,° only eighteen out of one hundred baby swimmers get colds in the winter. In contrast,° eighty-two out of one hundred nonswimmer babies get bad colds.

health care centers

baby beds, cribs / more or less

But

Kolya, a two-year-old boy, is the oldest "water baby" at one polyclinic in Russia. Every morning, he does chin-ups° on a bar. Then he jogs° with his father. Kolya's mother takes him to the swimming pool every day. He climbs the steps to the diving board,° then cheerfully°

happily

chin-ups

jogging

diving board

dives° into the water. He dives into the water many times and swims   jumps
until he is tired. When Kolya comes out of the pool, his mother gives
him a good rubdown.° Then she wraps him in a large towel and he   massage
rests. Nadya, his nine-month-old sister, also swims every day.

    "The earlier you start training babies, the better,"° says Char-   "It is good to teach babies
kovsky. "The more the babies exercise, the better they adapt to their   early,"
environment."° And the more they swim, the stronger they become.°   surroundings / grow
Kolya is a good example of Charkovsky's philosophy.° He is a strong,   ideas
independent boy who uses his hands and legs very well. "Swimming
is a wonderful exercise for everybody. It builds strong bodies and
sound° minds," says Charkovsky.   healthy

LEARNING ACTIVITIES

A. Check your comprehension

   1. Drawings 1 to 5 below represent paragraphs 1 to 5 in the reading. Select the drawing
     (A, B, or C) that *best* represents the ideas in each paragraph.

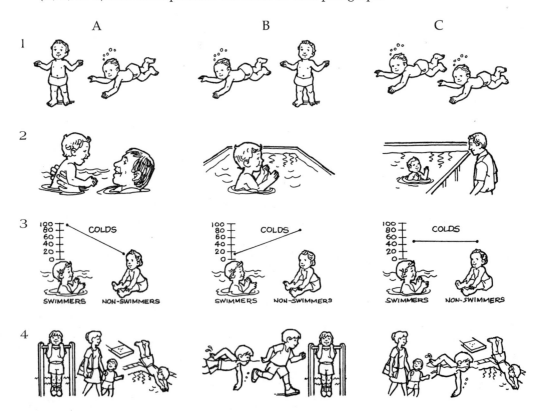

5

A   B   C

2. Study the instructions for teaching babies how to swim. Then number the instructions
in order from 1 to 6.

_____ Inhale again.

_____ Inhale slowly.

_____ Exhale slowly.

_____ Swim to the bottom of the pool.

_____ Hold your breath for two seconds.

_____ Swim to the surface of the water.

B. Increasing your word power

1. Study the word list below. Then circle the things that you take with you to the pool
or the beach.

goggles	a hat	a towel	a surf board
a cradle	a dress	lemonade	a diving board
sunglasses	a suit	a blanket	suntan lotion
sandwiches	a book	a magazine	an air mattress
an umbrella	?	a bathing suit	a cellular phone

2. Some swimmers can do these swimming strokes (movements):

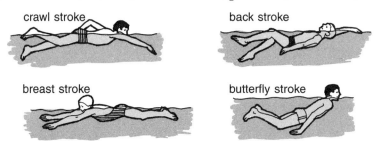

crawl stroke   back stroke

breast stroke   butterfly stroke

If you know how to swim, what strokes can you do?
"I can do the . . ."

3. Write the missing word.

"_____ babies" _____ filter _____ ski _____ polo

4. Nationalities: Complete the sentences below. Use a dictionary, if necessary.

EXAMPLE: Igor Charkovsky, a swimming instructor, is from <u>Russia</u>. He is <u>Russian</u>.

    a. Nadia Comaneci, a famous gymnast, is from Romania. She is _____.

    b. Sataharo Ohh, a well-known baseball player, is from Japan. He is _____.

    c. Martina Hingis, a tennis champion, was born in the Czech Republic. She is _____.

    d. Marcelo Salas is a great soccer player from Chile. He is _____.

    e. Monica Seles is a tennis player who was born in Yugoslavia. She is _____.

    f. Todd Eldridge, a silver-medal winner in ice skating, is from the United States. He is _____.

    g. Elvis Stoyko is an Olympic ice skater from Canada. He is _____.

    h. Alexander Popov, from Russia, is famous for his crawl stroke. He is _____.

    i. One of the finest Olympic divers is Fu Mingxia from China. She is _____.

    j. My name is _____ and I am from _____. I am _____.

5. New Words: Complete the table below using words from the reading. The words should mean about the same as the new word.

NEW WORD	SAME MEANING	OPPOSITE MEANING
EXAMPLE: relaxed	calm	nervous
a. great	_____	terrible
b. softly	_____	roughly
c. happily	_____	sadly
d. teacher	_____	student
e. baby	_____	adult
f. like	_____	dislike
g. top	_____	bottom
h. breathe out	_____	inhale

Now complete each sentence by using all three words in each word set above.

EXAMPLE: I love to go swimming in a lake. When the water is *calm*, I feel *relaxed*. But if it starts to rain, I get *nervous* and get out of the water.

a. Teaching babies to swim is a _____ idea. It's _____ that so many people can't swim today. "Swim first, walk later" is a _____ slogan.

b. When your baby gets out of the swimming pool, dry him or her _____ with a towel. Rub _____. If you rub the baby _____, you can hurt the child—so be careful!

c. "Most babies learn how to swim well," says Charkovsky _____. For example, little Kolya _____ dives into the pool and swims for an hour. When it's time to go home, he cries _____.

d. During the day, Charkovsky works as a/an _____; he teaches babies how to swim. At night, however, he studies. He is a graduate _____ at a university because he wants to be a better _____.

e. _____ should teach their _____ how to swim. Even small _____ who are only one month old can learn slowly.

f. Most babies _____ playing in the water. They _____ to splash water and play with their toys. But some infants _____ the water because they are afraid of it. Those children often grow up without learning how to swim.

g. Babies float up easily from the _____ to the _____ of a swimming pool. When they come to the _____ of the water, teach them to exhale, inhale, hold their breath, then dive down again.

h. "Teaching babies to swim is easy," says Charkovsky. "First, put them slowly near the surface of the water for a few seconds. When the infants _____, then _____ again, teach them not to _____ for two seconds. They will soon learn to hold their breath."

C. Reviewing articles

1. Read the following paragraph and complete it with **a, an,** or **some.**

Igor Charkovsky is _____ swimming instructor at _____ center for children. _____ babies go there every day to take swimming lessons with Igor. Kolya, _____ two-year-old boy, is the oldest student. He takes _____ swim with his mother and sister. They bring _____ air mattress and _____ toys to play with while they are in the pool.

2. Read the following paragraph, then complete it using **a** or **an** when you mean *one + noun,* or **the** when you mean a *definite person/persons, place, thing,* or *idea.*

Kolya is _____ oldest baby and _____ best swimmer at _____ childrens' center. Mr. Charkovsky, _____ instructor,

says that _____ pool is _____ only place where babies don't
cry. _____ slogan at the center is "Swim first, walk later." And that's
what most of _____ babies do.

D. Reviewing common verbs

Complete Nadya's schedule at the children's center. Write the *s* form of the verb.

8:00 A.M.	After getting up, Nadya *eats* breakfast. (to eat)
9:00 A.M.	Then she _____ children's TV programs. (to watch)
10:00 A.M.	She _____ to the swimming pool with her mom. (to go)
11:15 A.M.	She _____ lunch with her older brother. (to have)
12:00 P.M.	At noon Nadya _____ for an hour in her cradle. (to sleep)
1:00 P.M.	Afterward, she _____ other children play. (to watch)
3:00 P.M.	She _____ a snack at her grandma's house. (to have)
4:00 P.M.	She _____ back at home with her mother. (to be)
5:00 P.M.	Nadya's mother _____ her daughter supper. (to feed)
6:00 P.M.	Nadya _____ quietly with her brother. (to play)
6:15 P.M.	She _____ a short nap if she is tired. (to take)
7:00 P.M.	Her father _____ home from work. (to come)
7:30 P.M.	Nadya _____ to swim in her bath water. (to try)
8:00 P.M.	She _____ to bed with a bottle of milk. (to go)
8:15 P.M.	She _____ very tired and falls asleep. (to be)

E. Charkovsky's story

1. First, read the story below. Second, circle the verbs that are in the past tense. Third, list the infinitives of the verbs you circled (for example: **worked**—to work, **helped**—to help).

Charkovsky worked for many years to prove that animals who can swim develop faster than animals who do not swim. He began experimenting with cats, monkeys, and chickens. He noticed that they all dove into the water, swam around, and floated on the surface. Later, when they had baby kittens, monkeys, and chicks, their parents taught them how to swim. The young animals learned very fast. They became stronger and healthier than animals that do not learn how to swim.

2. Now complete Charkovsky's story. Write the past tense forms in the paragraph below.

Charkovsky also _____ (to have) a small baby girl, Tanya. She
_____ (to be) not very strong, but he _____ (to teach) her

how to float. After several lessons, Tanya _____ (to float) and
_____ (to swim) very well. She _____ (to become) stronger and
stronger, and she almost never _____ (to have) a cold. Today,
Tanya is a very pretty, healthy young woman.

F. Making comparisons

Study the comparisons in the last paragraph of the reading. Then complete the sentences
below with one of the words given in parentheses.

EXAMPLE: The more babies swim, the <u>stronger</u> they become. (stronger/weaker)

1. The more Kolya trains, the _____ he swims. (better/less)
2. The more Natasha jogs, the _____ she becomes. (healthier/shorter)
3. The less children exercise, the _____ they get sick. (more/less)
4. The _____ infants swim, the healthier they are. (less/more)
5. The _____ children scream, the more they enjoy themselves. (less/more)
6. The earlier babies learn to swim, the _____ swimmers they are. (better/more)

G. Conversations

1. **The power of water:** Since ancient times, many people have thought that water has
   special powers. Work with a conversation partner and talk about your ideas on the
   magic powers of water. The suggestions below can help you express your ideas.

a hot bath			
warm water			arthritis
salt water			your nerves
mineral water	is good for		bone diseases
mountain water			an upset stomach
ice-cold water			your general health
?			drinking on a hot day
			?

2. **Caring for children:** Ask a classmate the questions below. Discuss your ideas.

   a. In your country, do people pay a lot of attention to babies and small children?
      If so, how?
   b. Who usually takes care of the children?
   c. Do small children go to day care centers?
   d. Do little children learn how to swim. If so, where?

e. What kinds of toys do they have?

f. What kinds of games do they play?

g. What kinds of songs do they sing?

H. The swimming pigs

Read the paragraphs below. Then answer the questions by yourself or with other students in a small group.

Can Pigs Swim?

Some people think that pigs can't swim. But in Aquarena Springs in San Marcos, Texas, there are five pigs that swim like experts. Aquarena Springs is an entertainment park that has a "swimming pigs" show every day.

Every year the park buys and trains five white pigs to perform in the show. The instructor begins to train the pigs when they are only four days old. First, they learn how to swim. Then they learn how to dive into a large pool. They swim to their trainer, who gives them their reward: milk from a baby bottle!

All the pigs are called Ralph because people like that name. When the pigs get too fat, they have to leave the show. Then the park buys five more baby pigs, and the trainer begins to teach his new "students" again.

1. Do you think that the trainer knows about Charkovsky's ideas?

2. Why is it necessary to train five young pigs every year?

3. Why do you think they have *white* pigs at the park?

4. Why do the baby pigs learn how to dive so easily?

5. What would you name the five little pigs? Why?

VOCABULARY

Swim First, Walk Later

Nouns

baby / babies	diving board	moment	seconds	swimming pool
body / bodies	environment	morning	sister	swimmers
boy	example	mother	slogan	times
center	father	period	steps	towel
children	hands	philosophy	surface	water
children's centers	infant	polyclinics	swimming	water baby
colds	legs	pools	swimming instructor	winter
cradles	minds	rubdown		

Adjectives

bad	happy	longer	relaxed	strong / stronger
easy	healthy / healthier	many	sound	tired
every	independent	oldest	special	wonderful
good	large			

Verbs

adapt	cry	get	rest	teach
begin	dive	give	start	train
breathe	enjoy	jog	submerge	wait
build	exercise	learn	swim	walk
climb	exhale	lower	take	wrap
come out	float			

Adverbs

also	easily	first	later	very
cheerfully	fast	gently	so much	well
earlier				

Proper Nouns

Austria	Germany	Moscow	Russia	United States (USA)
England	Japan			

Expressions

in contrast	on the average	the more . . . the more	to do chin ups	to hold one's breath
nine-month-old	out of	to be afraid	to get a cold	two-year-old

2 An Orphanage[1] for Some Big Babies

In December 1995 a game warden° found Zoe, a robust° elephant born only two weeks ago. The baby elephant was wandering° in a village market near Kenya's Tsavo National Park. The badly decomposed° body of the infant's mother was found nearby. Zoe was driven by truck to a most unusual orphanage in Nairobi, run° by a woman named Daphne Sheldrick.

The wife of the late° David Sheldrick, founder and warden of Tsavo National Park, Daphne has worked with wild animals for over sixty years. In 1977 she opened the elephant orphanage at her home in Nairobi. There her trained staff° of eight replaces the baby elephants' families. So far the orphanage, which survives on charitable donations,° has saved twelve infants.

"Stressed baby elephants are very fragile,"° Daphne explains. "Often they have witnessed° the death of their families at the hands of ivory poachers° or irate° farmers whose crops have been trampled.° The baby elephants are so devastated with grief that some die of a broken heart."

As for Zoe, she was basically healthy, and once under Daphne's care she thrived.° The baby elephant drank six gallons of special formula° a day. Zoe soon became a confident and mischievous° youngster. After a year in the orphanage with the constant companionship of her human family, Zoe was weaned° and taken to a refuge at Tsavo National Park. There her favorite keepers will gradually introduce her to the ways of the wild, helping her to find food and water. Zoe spends nights with other elephant youngsters in a protected stockade.° It may take some years, but the ultimate aim—as with all the orphans—is to release her to a wild herd.

Daphne's dream for the future is to see "ivory remain banned,° all stockpiles destroyed, and no one to ever wear an ivory trinket."° There will always be competition for land, Daphne explains, but we can "protect elephants in the parks and give the young a chance."

protector of animals / strong
walking around

decayed
operated

deceased (dead)

co-workers
money given by people

weak
seen
thieves / angry / destroyed

lived well
modified milk / playful

removed from drinking milk

enclosure

made illegal
inexpensive souvenir

LEARNING ACTIVITIES

A. Check your comprehension

Complete each sentence below according to the reading selection.

1. The baby elephant was found by . . .
   a. a game warden.
   b. a male tourist.
   c. David Sheldrick.
   d. Daphne Sheldrick.

2. Zoe's mother was . . .
   a. at the orphanage.
   b. found dead.
   c. sad with grief.
   d. quite fragile.

3. Daphne Sheldrick lives in . . .
   a. a large elephant refuge.
   b. in a protected stockade.
   c. Nairobi, Kenya.
   d. Tsavo National Park.

4. Daphne . . .
   a. has stockpiles of ivory.
   b. is a stressed farmer.
   c. is an ivory poacher.
   d. protects baby elephants.

5. Daphne's orphanage . . .
   a. helps adult elephants.
   b. helps homeless children.
   c. is only for elephants.
   d. is quite rich today.

6. Some baby elephants die because . . .
   a. their parents kill them by accident.
   b. they do not have enough food to eat.
   c. they have seen their families killed.
   d. they receive poor care at the orphanage.

B. Increasing your word power

1. **Antonyms:** Circle the word that *best* completes each sentence. Then read aloud the completed sentences.

   a. When Zoe was found, she was a (robust/fragile) youngster.

   b. Some baby elephants die from (happiness/grief) after seeing their parents killed.

   c. At her special refuge near Nairobi, Daphne (destroys/protects) baby elephants like Zoe.

   d. Daphne and her (uneducated/trained) staff try to (save/destroy) as many elephant orphans as possible.

2. **Synonyms:** Read each sentence and replace the underlined word with one from the list. Then read the new sentence aloud.

banned	donations	mischievous	releases
co-workers	gradually	poachers	trinkets
companionship	grief		

   a. The elephant thieves cause a great deal of stress among elephants in Kenya. Those greedy people often make inexpensive souvenirs out of ivory, which are officially illegal in that country.

   b. Daphne's orphanage survives on charitable contributions. She and her staff take good care of their infant orphans there. Daphne frees the elephants when they are ready to live in the wild.

   c. Zoe had a great deal of friends with her human family. In time, she and most of the other baby elephants become playful youngsters.

C. What's in a name?

Some animals have special names in English. For example: Bambi, Donald Duck, Mickey Mouse, Dumbo the Flying Elephant.

1. Why do some people name animals in this way?

2. What are other special names for different animals, such as for household pets? Make a list of them and share your list with your classmates.

3. Do people in your country have special names for animals? If so, tell the class a few of those names. If you have pictures or drawings of the animals, bring the illustrations to class.

4. What are some popular names for boys in English? And for girls?

5. What are some common names for boys in your language? And for girls? Do you have a common name or an unusual one?

D. Animals everywhere!

1. Have you ever gone to a zoo or to a circus? If so, circle the names of the animals you saw there.

birds	snakes	lions	seals
giraffes	tigers	walruses	alligators
elephants	zebras	eagles	sea lions
turtles	rhinoceros	monkeys	penguins
deer	bears	dogs	horses

2. What is your favorite animal and why?

E. Preserving nature

1. Read each sentence below. Then write a number from 0 to 3 next to the sentence, depending on your feeling about it. Use the following scale:

0 = I strongly disagree   1 = I disagree   2 = I agree   3 = I strongly agree

a. _____ There are enough conservationists in the world.

   b. _____ We should preserve nature for everyone to enjoy.

   c. _____ It's better to see wildlife in a zoo rather than in nature.

   d. _____ It was a good idea to transport Zoe to the orphanage.

   e. _____ I walk or bicycle to school and/or to work quite often.

   f. _____ I enjoy walking in a park or hiking in the mountains.

   g. _____ I don't donate money to organizations that preserve nature.

   h. _____ I don't use a lot of water when I take a bath or shower.

   i. _____ I never throw trash on sidewalks or in streets.

   j. _____ Usually, I turn off the lights when I leave a room.

2. Add your numbers in (1) and divide the sum by 10. Then read the following chart.

AVERAGE	COMMENT
0–5	You are a wasteful person. If you help to preserve nature today, it will be there to enjoy tomorrow.
6–15	You are not very interested in preserving our environment. Please try to help protect nature. Then we all can enjoy life more.
16–25	You are concerned about the world we live in. You love nature and want to preserve it. Keep up your good attitude toward our environment!
26–30	You are a very special person because you really care about our environment. You deserve a gold medal for your love of nature and your positive attitude toward all living things.

3. Discuss with three or four classmates how and why you marked the sentences in (1) above.

F. Small group discussion

1. Pets: Do you like the idea of having pets? Do you have a pet at home? Use the questions below to express your ideas.

   a. Caring for a pet is a waste of time and money.

   b. A pet is a wonderful animal and friend.

   c. People should not live with animals.

   d. When I see a bird in a cage, I want to set it free.

   e. I don't understand why some people love their pets so much.

   f. A dog really is a person's best friend.

   g. I would (would not) like to have a pet because... I would like a/an
   _____. (_Or:_ I already have a pet. It's a _____ and its name is
   _____.)

2. **Caring:** Do you know of someone who tried to find a home for a person or an animal? Use the questions below to organize your story. Then tell it to the class.

   a. Who or what needed a home?

   b. Why did the person or animal need help?

   c. Who helped that person or animal?

   d. How did he or she help?

   e. How do you feel when you help people or animals?

   f. Have people ever helped you? If so, explain. How did you feel when they helped you?

G. Protecting nature

Imagine that you are trying to save a particular animal that may soon become extinct (no longer living on earth) if nothing is done to protect it.

   1. Make a short list of things you would do to protect the animal from extinction.

   2. Discuss your list with a classmate. Compare your lists.

   3. Meet with another group of two people, and compare your lists with theirs.

   4. Create an e-mail address for your particular defense group. If you can, create a Web site for your group.

   EXAMPLES: livegiants@livetusks.orphans.life
   http://www.livegiants.com

H. Forbidden jewels

If people continue to buy jewelry and souvenirs made from ivory, more elephants will die. Do the following activities with several of your classmates.

   1. Study the following list of clothing and accessories. Write the names of the animals that must die if people buy the items on the list.

   2. Write a slogan to defend each of these animals.

   3. Determine the fine, if any, for killing each animal.

suede jacket	silver fox fur coat	turtle shell hair combs
angora sweater	pigskin computer case	cashmere gloves and scarf
short seal jacket	heavy lamb-lined coat	leather motorcycle pants
snake cowboy boots	eel skin belt	crocodile skin purse

I. Research projects on the Internet

Apart from protecting natural habitats and ecosystems, each animal and plant has at least one positive effect on the environment. (Generally, you will find more than one positive effect.) Look for information about the effects of the six situations below. Then report this information to your class.

EXAMPLE: buffalo trampling the prairies
They help bury seeds in the ground.

1. ducks stirring a lake's bottom
2. elephants trampling the African savannah
3. goats uprooting plants from the ground
4. seals gorging on fish in the Arctic
5. birds feeding on the backs of rhinoceroses
6. salmon swimming upstream to deposit their eggs

VOCABULARY

An Orphanage for Some Big Babies

Nouns

aim	donations	game warden	orphanage	truck
body	dreams	grief	orphans	village
care	elephant	heart	poachers	warden
chance	farmers	herd	refuge	ways
companionship	formula	infant	staff	wife
competition	founder	ivory .	stockade	(the) wild
crops	future	keepers	stockpiles	(the) young
death	gallons	market	trinket	youngster

Adjectives

banned	decomposed	human	protected	trained
broken	devastated	irate	robust	ultimate
charitable	favorite	late	special	unusual
confident	fragile	mischievous	stressed	wild
constant	healthy			

Verbs

destroy	protect	run	thrive	wean
drive	release	save	trample	wear
explain	remain	spend	wander	witness
introduce	replace	survive		

Adverbs

badly   basically   gradually   nearby

Proper Nouns

Daphne Sheldrick   Kenya   Nairobi   Tsavo National Park   Zoe
David Sheldrick

Expressions

so far

Vocabulary Review
Unit I

A. Word sets

In each word set below, cross out the word that does *not* belong to it. Then explain why you crossed out the word in each set.

EXAMPLE: father / ~~infant~~ / sister / mother
                An *infant* is not a specific family member.

  1. Kenya / Nairobi / Russia / United States   _____

  2. hands / hearts / legs / minds   _____

  3. infants / babies / crops / children   _____

  4. healthy / stressed / strong / robust   _____

  5. to drive / to jog / to walk / to swim   _____

  6. warden / farmer / instructor / youngster   _____

  7. village / polyclinic / trinket / orphanage   _____

B. Reading for meaning

Read the selection below. Then complete the reading with appropriate words and phrases from the following list.

water baby, walks, protect, dives, to thrive, cheerfully, village, begins, confident, gives, sisters, poachers, healthy, swimming, jogs, elephant, trinkets, ivory, slogan, youngster, mischievous, mornings, rubdown, game warden

Saya and His Pet Elephant

Saya lives in a _____ in Kenya with his father, mother, and four _____. He is a _____ ten-year-old boy who enjoys _____ and playing with his pet _____ Babu. Babu is only two years old—just a _____—and is quite _____ one.

Several _____ each week Saya takes Babu to a river. Babu _____ quickly as Saya _____ beside his pet. When they reach the river, Saya _____ into the water. Then he _____ to splash Babu and washes him _____ with soap. Afterwards, Saya gives his pet a good _____. The young elephant is like a _____, and seems to _____ on all the attention his young master _____ him.

Saya knows that people must _____ the wild animals in Kenya. Someday he wants to become a _____ in Tsavo National Park. He is _____ that one day there will no longer be any _____ country and that visitors will no longer buy _____ made from elephant _____. Saya's _____ is "Come to Kenya, but take only photographs."

C. Which do you prefer?

Mark or write in the blank *one* preference to complete each sentence below. Then read aloud your preferences to a classmate. Your teacher may ask you to explain why you chose certain preferences.

1. I prefer to be . . .
   _____ healthy   _____ independent   _____

2. I would like to be more . . .
   _____ confident   _____ cheerful   _____

3. I like to . . .
   _____ swim   _____ walk   _____

4. I prefer . . .
   _____ exercising outside   _____ exercising inside   _____

5. It's more fun to . . .
   _____ save money   _____ spend money   _____

6. I like playing with . . .
   _____ animals   _____ children   _____

7. I'd like to visit . . .
   _____ Africa   _____ the United States   _____

8. I'd like to work in . . .
   _____ an orphanage   _____ a wildlife park   _____

9. I'd like to be . . .
   _____ an instructor   _____ a game warden   _____

10. I'd prefer to protect . . .
    _____ human orphans   _____ animal orphans   _____

D. Getting to know you

Ask a classmate the questions below. Write down his or her answers. When you finish, your classmate should ask you the same questions.

1. Do you exercise a lot? Do you jog? Do you do chin-ups? Which do you like most: walking or swimming? Why?

2. Do you have any pets? If so, tell me about them (for example, type of animal, its name, its personality). If you don't have any pets, would you like to have one? If so, what kind of pet?

3. Do you like children? If you have children, tell me about them. If you don't have children, would you like to have one or more? Why?

4. I will say some adjectives. Tell me if the adjectives describe you. Say "Yes," "No," or "It depends" (and explain on what it depends).

tired	happy	stressed	charitable
relaxed	healthy	confident	independent
strong			

E. Children and animals

Complete the crossword puzzle on the next page.

Children and animals

ACROSS

3. Health care centers
5. Run
6. Enclosure
8. Surroundings
12. A way of thinking
13. The end of life
14. Put under water

DOWN

1. Strong
2. Playful
4. Money given as charity
7. Sent back to the wild
9. Home for children without parents
10. Inexpensive souvenirs
11. Healthy
12. Where people swim

UNIT II

FAMILY TIES

3 Finding Yourself on Your Family Tree[1]

[1]A *family tree* is a chart that shows how family members are related. For example, look at the family tree in Exercise B, page 28.

Finding out about your family history is a very personal experience. It takes time and effort° but it is fascinating and fun.

Most people who study their family history say the same thing: they learn a lot about themselves. Dr. Mary Matossian teaches a college course in family history. She says, "Every family has unique° ways of dealing with life. All this has a powerful effect because it makes us the kind of people we are."

A family history shows patterns of behavior° that often repeat themselves in every generation. For example, if your grandmother Marianne was a weak, nervous person and your grandfather John was strict,° probably your mother and father follow the same pattern—or the exact opposite. Whatever the pattern, it affects the way children feel about marriage and close relationships. If you know the pattern, it is easier to change it, if you wish. A study of three generations is enough to find the repeating patterns.

Here are the five suggestions to start a study of a family history:

1. Begin with the side of the family that you do not know very well.[2]
2. Talk to as many relatives as possible.
3. Find out the family secrets from your relatives.
4. Study letters, diaries,[3] scrapbooks,[4] and pictures for clues.°
5. Try to study in detail the periods° when important family changes took place.°

The artists always say it best. William Faulkner wrote, "The past is never dead. It's not even past."

°work

°different

°ways in which people do things

°demanding

°information that helps solve problems / times

°happened

---

[2]There are two sides of every family: your father's relatives and your mother's relatives. When you study your family history, you must study both your *father's side* and your *mother's side*.

[3]A *diary* is a book in which people write about their experiences, thoughts, and feelings.

[4]A *scrapbook* contains a person's photographs, cards, letters, and newspaper articles that mean something special to him or her.

LEARNING ACTIVITIES

A. Check your comprehension

Read each sentence below. Decide whether the sentence is true or false according to the reading selection. If it is false, say why.

1. If your grandparents are friendly, you and your parents will be friendly, too.
2. Studying your family tree is easy.
3. When you study your family history, you will also learn a lot about yourself.
4. One good way to study your family history is to talk with relatives.
5. All families have more or less the same behavior patterns.

B. A family tree

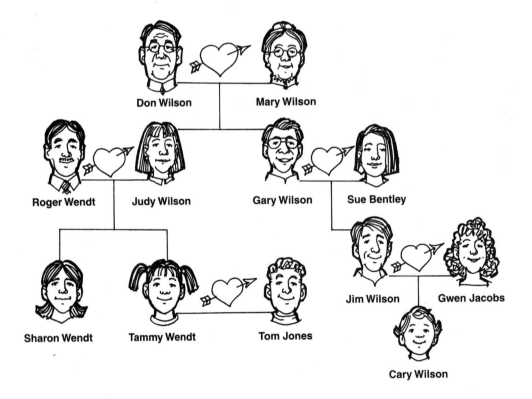

The family chart above shows three generations. Study the following vocabulary list, then complete the sentences below.

Vocabulary

parents	daughter	grandson	cousin
husband	grandparents	granddaughter	brother-in-law
wife	grandfather	brother	sister-in-law
son	grandmother	sister	

EXAMPLE: David Murphy is the <u>husband</u> of Judy Wilson.

1. Don and Mary Wilson have been married for fifty years. They are Jim Wilson's _____.

2. Jim Wilson is Gary Wilson's _____.

3. Sharon and Tammy Wendt are the _____ of Roger Wendt and Judy Wilson, and the _____ of Don and Mary Wilson.

4. When Tom Jones marries Tammy Wendt, their children's last name will be _____.

5. Tammy Wendt and Jim Wilson are _____.

6. Judy Wilson and Sue Bentley are _____.

7. In twenty years, if Cary Wilson marries a man named John Bedford, then Cary's new name will be _____.

C. Using idioms

1. Answer the following questions in complete sentences.

   a. Which *side of your family* do you know best?
   b. How do you *feel about* marriage?
   c. When you have a big problem, how do you *deal with* it?
   d. What *takes time and effort* to do well?
   e. Does divorce *have an effect on* children? What effect?
   f. Where do weddings *take place* in your country?
   g. Can you describe your family tree *in detail*?

2. Write a sentence using each italicized idiom in (1) above.

D. Crossword puzzle

Complete the crossword puzzle on the next page by using words from the reading selection. Use the vocabulary list on page 35 as a guide.

ACROSS

4. Each _____ is different from the previous generation.

7. I can't _____ my book. Have you seen it?

8. I don't understand. Please _____ what you said, sir.

10. Abdul and I have the _____ name; we both are called Abdul.

11. Russia, China, and the United States are the most _____ countries in the world.

13. I have no relatives; they are all _____.

14. Do you want this piece of cake or _____ piece of pie?

15. Everyone must study _____ and geography in school.

16. I don't like that _____ of person. I like generous people.

18. Come _____ my house tomorrow, Soo Lin.

20. Visit me, _____ you have time, John.

21. If you make any _____ in your plans, please tell me.

23. _____ me, please. I know the way to the museum.

25. Last night I _____ my wife to dinner at a good Chinese restaurant.

DOWN

1. I study English _____ night except on Saturday nights.

2. _____ your pants, Kenny. They're so dirty.

3. This gift is _____ you, Basil.

5. Christina is on my _____ of the family.

6. Yesterday I _____ you a letter.

9. This morning I _____ missed my bus to school. I'm glad that I didn't.

10. If you want to speak English well, you must _____ every day.

12. Israel is a _____ country to visit.

17. My _____ contains many old pictures and letters.

19. My uncle is the brother _____ my mother or father.

22. A girl always likes to be _____ to her boyfriend.

24. I don't have my book because I lost _____ yesterday.

E. Word sets

Words can be related to each other like members of a family.

1. In each word set, cross out the word that is *not* related to the other three words. Then explain why the three remaining words belong to the same "family."

    EXAMPLE: sister/mother/~~friend~~/father   A *friend* is not a relative.

    a. letter/diary/note/period   _____

    b. weak/nervous/unique/sick   _____

    c. repeat/know/understand/learn   _____

    d. powerful/strong/weak/important   _____

    e. change/scrapbook/pictures/letters   _____

    f. experience/people/children/Grandma   _____

    g. English/geography/history/marriage   _____

2. Write *one* word from *each* word set in (1) that best completes each sentence.

    EXAMPLE: My <u>mother</u> was in the hospital for two days before I was born.

    a. When you study _____, you learn the names of political and religious leaders.

    b. I like to put interesting things such as stamps, coins, and postcards in my _____.

    c. My friend, Manivong, is _____ because she is the only person I know who speaks Laotian, English, French, and some German.

    d. Yesterday I had a wonderful _____: I rode in a hot air balloon.

    e. Every day I write my thoughts and feelings in my _____.

    f. It's very _____ to practice English every day.

    g. I'm sorry, I didn't understand. Would you please _____ what you said?

F. Who's who?

Each of us has different interests. For example, some people like sports, others like to read; some people want large families, others prefer to stay single. In each of the following sentences, write in the name of a classmate or another person you know. Then sit with a classmate and read aloud the names you wrote in the sentences.

EXAMPLE: <u>Irma</u> cooks very well.

1. _____ studies a lot.   **6.** _____ has visited Europe.

2. _____ plays the guitar.   **7.** _____ likes people a lot.

3. _____ cooks very well.

4. _____ watches lots of TV.

5. _____ surfs the Internet.

8. _____ plays soccer well.

9. _____ is getting married.

10. _____ wants to own a business.

G. Getting information

Ask another student the questions below. Choose a word or phrase from each column to form at least four questions in each set.

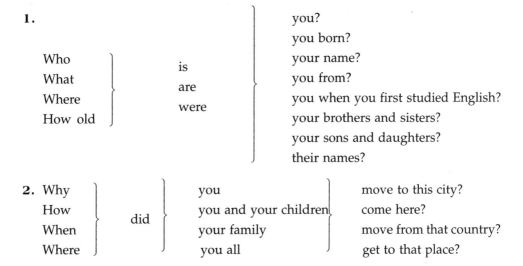

1.

Who			you?
What	is		you born?
Where	are		your name?
How old	were		you from?

you when you first studied English?
your brothers and sisters?
your sons and daughters?
their names?

2.

Why		you	move to this city?
How	did	you and your children	come here?
When		your family	move from that country?
Where		you all	get to that place?

H. Matching

Match each relative with his or her characteristics.

1. ____ me
2. ____ my grandfather
3. ____ my aunt
4. ____ my son/daughter
5. ____ my grandmother
6. ____ my mother
7. ____ my father
8. ____ my nephew/niece
9. ____ my ?

a. strict (wants someone to do something in a certain way)
b. troubled (has many problems; is worried)
c. strong (full of energy; very healthy)
d. generous (gives people many things out of love)
e. nervous (makes people angry or excited)
f. nice (pleasant, charming)
g. kind (loving; friendly)
h. weak (not strong or healthy; sickly)
i.   ?

I. You and your family

Ask a classmate the questions below. When you finish, your classmate should ask you the same questions.

1. Who is stricter: your father or your mother?
2. Who is the most intelligent person in your family?
3. Who is lazier: you or your brother/sister?
4. Who works the most in your family?
5. Who speaks English the best in your family? Why?
6. Which person do you feel closest to in your family? Why?

J. Describing your family

Write a short composition about your family.

First paragraph: My father's name is / was _____ and my mother's name is / was _____. My mother comes / came from _____.
(country)
and my father comes / came from _____. When my parents got married, they lived first in _____ for _____ years. They follow / They don't follow the same pattern as my grandparents because . . .

Second paragraph: I was born on _____ in the town / city of
(date)
_____ in _____. My family and I lived there for _____
(country)
years. We now / still live in _____.

Third paragraph [for single persons]: I am single. I live alone / with _____.
I work at / for _____ and I study English at _____. Someday
(company)
I want to . . . but right now I have to . . .

Third paragraph [for married persons]: I am married. I live with my family in _____. My husband's / wife's name is _____. We have _____ child / children. (We don't have children.) I work at / for _____ and I study English at _____. Someday I want to. . . .
(company)
but right now I have to . . .

K. "Relatively" speaking

Think of a certain tree you like. Using the vocabulary from this chapter, describe the character of that tree and compare it to a relative.

EXAMPLE: I love poplar trees because they are very tall and thin like my grandfather. Poplars line the fields and look very serious when they teach discipline to the other trees, just like my Grandma. Poplars are not very strong like my cousin Annette.

Common trees: oaks, pines, chestnuts, sycamores, plantains, maples, magnolias, willows, spruces, alders

VOCABULARY

Finding Yourself on Your Family Tree

Nouns

behavior	experience	letters	periods	scrapbooks
charts	generation	marriage	persons	secrets
clues	grandfather	member	pictures	side
diaries	grandmother	opposite	relationships	study
effect	history	past	relatives	suggestions
effort	kind	pattern		

Adjectives

close	enough	fun	powerful	unique
dead	exact	nervous	repeating	weak
easier	fascinating	personal	strict	

Verbs

affect	find out	show	start	wish
deal with	feel about			

Proper Nouns

William Faulkner	Mary Matossian

Expressions

because	in detail	to take place	to take time	whatever the . . .

4 The Food of Love

When I was a child, the traditional Sunday lunch in the Stellino household was a simple affair.° *event*

One Sunday, I remember my mother preparing pasta with lima beans and Swiss chard[1]—a family favorite. As soon as the dessert was finished, my brother Mario and I sprang° from our chairs to get to the *got up quickly* soccer stadium. Our home team, Palermo, was playing against our hated rivals° from Catania.[2] We bolted° from the house, leaving our *competitors / left quickly* parents to a quiet afternoon together.

When we arrived at the stadium, I realized I had left the tickets at home. So I ran the twelve long blocks home as fast as my feet could carry me. As I entered the front door, huffing and puffing,° I heard a *out of breath* romantic song that I recognized as an oldie from my parents' dating days. I quickly made my way to my room, grabbed the tickets, and headed out.° As I passed the living room's door, I noticed that it was *left* cracked open. My child's curiosity overcame my anxiety° to get back *nervousness* to the stadium: I softly pushed the door to peek° inside. *look carefully*

In the soft shadows of the living room—our *salotto*—I saw my parents in each other's arms, gently dancing to the music. My mother was wearing yellow gloves for washing dishes, but her head rested against my father's shoulder.

Feeling as guilty° as an uninvited guest, I quietly closed the door *at fault* behind me, and, this time, tiptoed° out of the house. I don't remember *walked on my toes* who won the soccer game, but I will always remember my parents young, in love, and dancing in each other's arms.

---

[1]*Swiss chard* is a green vegetable similar to spinach but much larger.
[2]*Palermo* and *Catania* are cities on the island of Sicily in Italy.

LEARNING ACTIVITIES

A. Check your comprehension

1. Complete the following sentences by choosing the correct word or phrase in parentheses.

   a. The author of the reading lived in (Palermo / Catania / another town).

   b. He and his brother played (soccer / football / baseball).

   c. The Stellino boy returned home (to get some tickets / to see his parents / to eat lunch).

   d. When the boy got home, his parents were (dancing / washing dishes / listening to music).

   e. An oldie is (a song from long ago / an interesting game / an elderly person).

2. Answer the following questions based on your own opinion.

   a. Why did the Stellino boy tiptoe around his own house?

   b. How old do you think he and his brother were in the reading?

   c. Why do you think the title of this reading is "The Food of Love"?

B. Increasing your word power

1. Write at least one word or expression associated with each word below. Then write at least ten sentences using this new vocabulary.

a. tiptoe	d. game	g. front door	j. lima beans
b. huffing	e. grab	h. dating days	k. yellow gloves
c. peek	f. dance	i. home team	l. made my way

2. Children never forget the magical moments when they discover something new. Complete the following statements to express what you saw or discovered when you were a child.

   a. I stopped for a moment and I peeked inside. I saw . . .

   b. The window was cracked open so I . . .

   c. As I passed the big room I heard . . .

   d. I opened my eyes and I . . .

   e. The house was very quiet but I heard . . .

   f. When I saw . . . in each other's arms I knew . . .

C. I'm in a hurry!

Many young people are not very patient. Tell the story of this young girl by changing the boldfaced verbs into their past forms.

EXAMPLE: I **have** a basketball game, so I **spring** from my chair as soon as lunch **is** over.

I **had** a basketball game, so I **sprang** from my chair as soon as lunch **was** over.

On a cool afternoon in November, as soon as lunch **is** finished, I **spring** from my chair to get to a computer group meeting with my classmates. We **are** competing against a rival group to see who **can** find the best Web sites for our class, Introduction to World Business. When the bus **gets** to our stop, we **bolt** from our seats, upsetting the driver because he **says** "teenagers make too much noise."

When we **arrive** at the computer center, I **realize** that I **am** so absent-minded that I **leave** my student identity card at home. Instead of taking the bus again, I **run** home twelve blocks as fast as my feet **can** carry me. As I **enter** the front door, I **hear** my younger sister on the phone singing an oldie in her bedroom. I **don't** have much time to think, so I quickly **make** my way to my room and **grab** my ID card.

As I **leave** I **can** hear my sister still singing over the phone, but I **notice** that her voice **is** even sweeter now. I **want** to get a closer look, so I **push** open her door a bit and **peek** inside. To my surprise, she **is** not on the phone. She **is** singing to one of her dolls!

I **leave** the house smiling and **begin** running to my meeting for the second time.

D. My family ties

Tell a classmate something about your family, using the incomplete paragraphs below to guide your conversation. Your teacher may ask you to complete the paragraphs in writing once you have finished the speaking activity.

As a child, I had a (small / medium-size / large) family. My father's name is / was _____, and he worked as a / an _____. My mother's name (occupation)
is / was _____ , and she worked as a / an _____. I had / have _____ brother(s) and _____ sisters. Their names are / were . . . (number)
We lived in (a house / an apartment) in _____, _____ where (town)   (country)
I grew up.

I also have grandparents. I had/have _____ grandfathers whose (number)
names are / were . . . They worked as . . . I also had / have _____ grand- (number)
mothers whose names are / were . . . They worked as . . .

E. Then and now

As we grow up, our likes and dislikes change. Complete the chart below by naming some people, places, food, and pastimes that you liked as a child, and those you now enjoy as an adult.

	AS A CHILD	AS AN ADULT
PEOPLE		
My best friend	_____	_____
A special guest	_____	_____
PLACES		
My special place	_____	_____
A romantic location	_____	_____
FOOD		
A delicious main dish	_____	_____
My favorite dessert	_____	_____
PASTIMES		
My favorite sport	_____	_____
A rival team	_____	_____
A really great game	_____	_____

Now speak with a classmate about your childhood compared with your adulthood, based on the names that you wrote in the chart above.

EXAMPLE: When I was a child my best friend was Jenny, but now it is . . .

F. Using numbers

There are many ways to express numbers besides using numerals. For example, age-group names are sometimes used to place people in broad age categories. Here are some common ones:

- Infants, babies
- Toddlers (1–3 years old)
- Kids, children
- Teenagers, teen years (13–19 years old)
- People in their twenties (20s)
  He is twenty-something.
- People in their thirties (30s)
  She is thirty-something.

English speakers use ordinal numbers in schools to categorize students by grade level, and to classify something.

GRADE LEVELS	RATINGS
first-graders	first-class pasta dish
second-graders	second-class restaurant
third-graders	third-class bus fare

1. Write the names of six friends and relatives of all ages along with their age group or approximate age. Then note their occupation, business, or profession by giving a rating in the example below.

2. Write a statement describing each person by using at least two number expressions per person.

> EXAMPLE: My aunt Daniça is in her forties, but she says she is in her thirties. She is a first-class dentist.

G. Food events

1. In all cultures, certain foods tend to be related to important events. Describe in simple terms the foods that you associate with those moments. Afterward, describe a few of the dishes to a classmate.

    a. New Year's celebration
    b. the birth of a child
    c. a wedding
    d. moving into a new house
    e. a funeral
    f. a religious celebration

2. Ask a classmate about his or her eating habits, using the questions below, then he or she will ask you the same questions.

    a. What do you eat when you are: sad / in a hurry / sick with a cold / too warm in summer?
    b. What do you drink after eating / running / sleeping / dancing?
    c. What kinds of bread do you like?
    d. Who prepares food in your family? Is that a traditional custom?
    e. What is one dish or kind of food that you could eat every day / every week?

H. Oldies, but goodies

As adults we all remember many songs from our teenage years. These songs are called "oldies."

1. Make a list of four or five oldies that you liked or that your parents like.

2. Ask someone about twenty years older than you to name an oldie that he or she enjoyed as a teenager.

3. Compare your lists with those of a classmate.

4. *Optional*: Bring one or more oldies to class and play it for your classmates. How many people can sing it along with you?

I. Looking back

The author of the reading at the beginning of this chapter wrote about a special event that happened on one day when he was a boy. Now it's your turn. Think about a special day when you were still a child and something happened that you will always remember. Here are several questions to ask yourself:

1. Exactly what happened on that day?

2. How old were you when it occurred?

3. When and where did the event happen?

4. To whom did the event happen?

Make some notes based on your thoughts. Then write a 200-word composition about that day in your childhood.

BEGIN LIKE THIS: When I was about _____ years old, on a cold winter day in our city of _____, . . .

VOCABULARY

The Food of Love

Nouns

affair	dessert	guest	lunch	shadows
afternoon	dishes	head	mother	shoulder
anxiety	door	home team	music	soccer game
blocks	family	house	oldie	soccer stadium
brother	father	household	parents	song
chairs	feet	lima beans	pasta	Sunday
child	food	living room	rivals	Swiss chard
curiosity	front door	love	room	tickets
dating days	gloves			

Adjectives

cracked open	hated	romantic	traditional	yellow
favorite	long	simple	uninvited	young
guilty	quiet	soft		

Verbs

arrive	feel	leave	prepare	rest against
bolt from	finish	notice	puff	run
carry	grab	overcome	push	spring from
close	head out	pass	realize	tiptoe
dance	hear	peek	recognize	wash
enter	huff	play	remember	wear

Adverbs

always	inside	quickly	quietly	softly
gently				

Proper Nouns

Catania	Mario	Palermo	Stellino

Expressions

at home	in love	to make one's way

Vocabulary Review
Unit II

A. Word sets

In each word set below, cross out the word that does *not* belong to it. Then explain why you crossed out the word in each set.

EXAMPLE: ~~shoulder~~ / mother / brother / father
           A *shoulder* is a body part, not a relative.

1. oldie / music / pattern / song   _____
2. effort / team / soccer / stadium   _____
3. William / Mario / Mary / Palermo   _____
4. gently / softly / quickly / quietly   _____
5. charts / lunch / letters / scrapbooks   _____
6. pasta / Swiss chard / side / dessert   _____

B. Reading for meaning

After reading the selection below, fill in the blanks with appropriate words and phrases from the following list.

curiosity, pasta, takes, study, powerful, letters, afternoon, history, find out, relatives, scrapbooks, members, parents, generations, child, affairs, fascinating, romantic, marriage

A Popular Hobby

A popular hobby among Americans is the _____ of their family _____. They want to _____ as much as possible who their _____ were. They begin with their _____, then ask others about people related to them over _____.

The basic motivation behind this search is _____. Was Uncle George a _____ man? How many love _____ did he have? Why did Grandma Rose like _____ so much? Was she an only _____? Why did Aunt Bea and Uncle Harry break up their _____?

The answers to these questions may be found by reading old _____, looking at hundred-year-old _____, and talking to many family _____. Of course, this hobby _____ lots of time.

One can't learn all the information in just one _____. But with patience and determination, this hobby is both _____ and _____.

C. Which do you prefer?

Mark or write in the blank *one* preference to complete each sentence below. Then read aloud your preferences to a classmate. Your teacher may ask you to explain your choices.

1. I prefer . . .

   _____ traditional things   _____ modern things   _____

2. I like listening to . . .

   _____ oldies   _____ romantic songs   _____

3. My favorite sport is . . .

   _____ soccer   _____ baseball   _____

4. It's fun to . . .

   _____ play soccer   _____ dance   _____

5. I like . . .

   _____ pasta   _____ rich desserts   _____

6. During the week, I usually have lunch . . .

   _____ at home   _____ at school   _____

7. On Sunday afternoons, I like to . . .

   _____ study English   _____ play music   _____

8. I prefer to study in . . .

   _____ my living room   _____ my bedroom   _____

9. I love . . .

   _____ my grandparents   _____ my parents   _____

10. For me, marriage is . . .

    _____ romantic   _____ fascinating   _____

D. Getting to know you

Ask a classmate the questions below. Write down his or her answers. When you finish, your classmate should ask you the same questions.

1. Do you have an album with photographs of your family? Where is it? When did you begin your photo album? If you do not have a photo album, would you like to begin one? Why?

2. Do you have a scrapbook? What does it contain? If you do not have a scrapbook, would you like to begin one? Why?

3. Who does the dishes in your household? Who cooks? Do you like pasta? Have you tasted Swiss chard? What kinds of foods do you like?

4. I will read aloud some adjectives. Tell me if they describe you. Say "Yes," "No," or "It depends" (and explain on what it depends).

fun	simple	nervous	powerful
weak	unique	romantic	traditional
quiet			

E. All in the family

Complete the crossword puzzle on the next page.

All in the family

ACROSS

2. A book of collectible items
6. A way of acting or conducting oneself
7. Nervousness
8. The opposite of "future"
10. Very interesting
12. The opposite of "forget"
14. Softly
15. Times or intervals

DOWN

1. For example: spaghetti, macaroni
2. Kinds of advice
3. A legal bond between a man and a woman
4. People who are related to you
5. Competitors
9. A famous American writer
11. The color of the sun
13. Want or desire

UNIT **III**

FOREIGN TRAVEL

Taufa'ahau Tupou IV, King of Tonga

5 The King and I

My fale *at the Good Samaritan Inn*

Two of my greatest interests in life are bicycle touring and meeting people from other countries. Last March I spent a two-week vacation on Tongatapu,[1] a lovely° island in the South Pacific Ocean. Every morning after breakfast I left my one-room *fale*[2] at the Good Samaritan Inn. Dressed in shorts, T-shirt, and sandals,° I rode my bicycle to different villages on the island.

beautiful

sandals

In one village I met two young men who were Mormon missionaries.[3] The short, muscular man was from Tonga, and his tall, thin partner came from Western Samoa.

"How do you like my country?" the Tongan asked me with a big smile.

"I love it!" I answered. "This island is so beautiful. And the people are so friendly here."

"Thank you," my Tongan friend replied. "By the way, do you know that we have two kings here in Tonga?"

"Two kings? I don't understand," I said confused.

"There is our heavenly king,° God the Father. And our earthly king, King Taufa'ahau Tupou IV."

Jesus Christ

I assured° him that as a Christian, I already knew the first king. But I was eager to meet the other one: the King of Tonga. Before leaving home, I wrote several letters to request an audience with His Majesty,° but I never received a reply. To my surprise I soon learned that Edwin, the owner of the Good Samaritan Inn, was the personal secretary of the King Taufa'ahau.

told him honestly

ask to visit the king

Naturally I went to the Royal Palace office to visit Edwin. When I requested an audience with King Taufa'ahau, I mentioned to° Edwin that I was staying at his resort. He smiled and said, "Oh, you're staying at the Good Samaritan? I'll see what I can do."

told

[1]*Tongatapu* is the main island in the Kingdom of Tonga. The capital of that country, Nuka'lofa, is located on Tongatapu.
[2]A *fale* is a thatched house with simple furniture.
[3]Missionaries are people who are sent abroad to spread religious beliefs.

Hand-painted tapa *in my* fale

armored truck

The day before I left Tonga, Edwin arranged for me to meet King Taufa'ahau at a gymnasium where His Majesty exercised. At precisely° 2:30 in the afternoon, the king arrived in a green armored truck.° Two policemen on motorcycles and eight bodyguards° in a van escorted the truck to the entrance of the gym. When one bodyguard opened the door of the truck, His Majesty stepped out. This seventy-eight-year-old gentleman was a giant:° he stood at six feet, five inches (1.96 meters), and weighed more than 350 pounds (157.5 kilos). He wore a white T-shirt, baggy° shorts, and size twenty sneakers.° I thought, "Now that's a king!"

    At first, the king's bodyguards would not allow me to approach His Majesty closely, so I was unable to take good photographs of the king. During one of his rest periods, however, the king noticed that I was taking pictures of him. Suddenly, he whispered° something to his personal physician. The doctor approached me and said, "The king would like to speak with you. Please come."

    I took my camera quickly and walked slowly over to the king who was resting comfortably in a chair. I knelt down on one knee and, extending° my right hand, introduced myself. "Hello, Your Majesty. I'm Jim Hendrickson from the United States. I'm so honored and pleased to meet you." The king shook my hand and smiled.

    I continued kneeling at the foot of His Majesty's chair while we chatted like good friends. During our brief conversation I asked the king if I could take his picture. He graciously° granted my request.° Trembling° with excitement, I set my camera on autofocus, zoomed in very closely on His Majesty's massive° head and torso,° and clicked away. I thought to myself, "At last, I have met the King of Tonga!"

exactly

people who protect others

very tall person

loose / tennis shoes

spoke quietly

holding out

kindly / gave me permission
Shaking
large / upper part of the body

LEARNING ACTIVITIES

A. Check your comprehension

1. Circle the word that best completes each sentence, according to the reading. Then answer the questions and explain the reasons for your answers.

    a. The author visited Tonga to (work / relax / study).

    b. The young Mormon missionaries were (men / women).

    c. The author seemed to (like / dislike) Tonga.

    d. The king's secretary (helped / did not help) the author.

    e. The author (spoke / exercised / laughed) with the king.

    f. The king seemed to (like / dislike) the author.

    g. The king's physician seemed (angry / intelligent / kind).

2. Write the names of the following people and places mentioned in the reading.

PEOPLE

    a. the "earthly" king   _____

    b. the "heavenly" king   _____

    c. the king's secretary   _____

    d. the author of the reading _____

PLACES

    a. a resort on Tongatapu   _____

    b. the ocean around Tonga   _____

    c. where the author lives   _____

    d. where the author slept   _____

    e. where the king exercises   _____

    f. where the secretary works _____

B. Now and then

Go back to the reading and circle all the verbs that describe an action in the past. Be sure you know the present tense form of the verbs. After reviewing those verb forms, complete the sentences below by writing the past form of the verb in italics.

EXAMPLE: My friend is not tall; he *stands* only five feet high. But the king of Tonga <u>stood</u> six feet, five inches.

1. Kings usually ride in luxury cars, but the author _____ a bicycle.

2. Instead of taking his Mercedes Benz to the gym, the king _____ his armored car.

3. The king shakes hands with many visitors, but when he _____ Jim's hand it was very special to Jim.

4. Jim often thinks of visiting China, but he _____ that the South Pacific was more interesting.

5. Jim is spending some time in Africa now, but last year he _____ his winter vacation in Tonga.

6. Missionaries usually meet very different people on their trips, but in Tonga they _____ an unusual tourist who rode a bicycle.

7. To leave home to see the world is not easy. But when Jim _____ Tonga it was also difficult because he had made many friends there.

8. Jim had to kneel when speaking with the king. After their conversation, he could not remember how long he _____ in front of His Majesty because he was so excited.

9. The Mormon missionaries know the heavenly father well, and Jim _____ him well, too.

10. Jim wears baggy pants and sneakers when he wants to be comfortable. But he didn't think a king _____ the same kind of clothes.

C. Increasing your word power

1. What does a king or queen of a country really need to have? Answer this question by writing a number before each noun below, using the scale.

   0 = Not important   1 = Important   2 = Very important

_____ bicycle	_____ motorcycle	_____ sandals
_____ bodyguards	_____ office	_____ secretary
_____ camera	_____ physician	_____ sneakers
_____ friends	_____ resort	_____ truck
_____ gymnasium	_____ rest periods	_____ van

2. Now complete the sentences below by using the nouns above. Sometimes you may need to add an -s to the nouns that you use. Write your sentences in your notebook.

   EXAMPLES: I have (a / an / a pair of / many) _____.
   I have a bicycle. I have many friends.

   a. I have (a / an / a pair of / many) _____.
   b. I need (a / an / a pair of / many) _____.

c. I don't have (a / an / a pair of / many) _____ .

d. I don't need (a / an / a pair of / many) _____ .

D. Dressed for the occasion

Were you surprised that kings sometimes wear baggy shorts when they exercise? First, list the pieces of clothing mentioned in the reading. Then write what you wear to the following places.

> EXAMPLE: at a reception   I wear good clothes and shoes.

1. in class   **4.** at the beach

2. at the gym   **5.** at a wedding

3. at the movies   **6.** going out with friends

E. Identities

After reading the complete sentences below, write some information about yourself. Use the English or the metric system.

1. The King of Tonga is seventy-eight years old. He is six feet, five inches (1.9 meters) tall, and weighs about 350 pounds (159.5 kilos). I am _____ years
   (number)
   old, I am _____ feet (meters) tall, and I weigh about _____
   (number)
   pounds/kilos.

2. The Tongan missionary is short and muscular. The Western Samoan missionary is tall and thin. I am _____ and _____ .
   (trait)   (trait)

3. The missionaries are Mormon. The author is Christian. I am _____ .
   (religion)
   (I don't have a religion.)

4. Edwin works as a secretary in the Royal Palace office. I work as a _____ in / at _____ .
   (profession)   (place of work)

5. The author gets around by bicycle. The King of Tonga gets around in an armored truck. I get around (by bus / on foot / in my car / ?).

6. The King of Tonga exercises in a gymnasium in the afternoon. I exercise in / at _____ in the _____ . (I don't exercise.)
   (place)   (time)

7. The author spent a two-week vacation in Tonga. I spent a _____ vaca-
   (time)
   tion in _____ . (I didn't have a vacation this year.) Someday I'd like to
   (place)
   spend a _____ vacation in _____ .
   (time)   (place)

F. Welcome to the South Pacific!

Go to the library and look at a large map of the South Pacific Ocean. Choose one island country, like Tonga, or a single island in that country, like Tongatapu. Do some research about that country or island, then write a short report about your findings. Your teacher may also ask you to make a short oral report in class based on your research.

Here are some suggestions about what to look for in your research.

1. Other islands or island countries nearby
2. The name of the capital city of your island country
3. How many people live in that country
4. The language(s) they speak there
5. How the people earn a living (make money)
6. The most popular religions in the country or on the island
7. Two or three other interesting things you learned from your research

G. My island dream

Suppose you could visit a lovely island in the South Pacific Ocean. Speak with a classmate by answering the following questions. If possible, use a map of that region.

1. What island or group of islands would you visit?
2. Why would you visit that particular place?
3. Who would go along with you there?
4. What would you take with you on your trip?
5. How would you travel to that place?
6. What would you wear every day?
7. How would you get around the island or island group?
8. Where would you stay over there? For how long?
9. What kinds of activities would you do there?
10. What souvenirs would you bring home?

H. If I were a king or queen

Kings and queens have a great deal of money, power, and freedom to do what they want. What would you do if you were a king or queen? Write your answers to that question by completing the following sentences.

If I were a king or queen, I would have . . .

I would like . . .

I would help . . .

I would live . . .

I would travel . . .

I would . . .

I would not . . .

I. Now that's a king!

The seventy-eight-year-old king of Tonga certainly is an impressive gentleman. Using the model below, describe an important person in your country or in your family. Write the description in your notebook. Begin like this:

At precisely . . . in the afternoon, . . . arrived . . . Two friends / relatives / policemen . . . accompanied him / her to the entrance of . . . When . . . opened the door of the . . . , . . . stepped out. The . . .-year-old gentleman / lady was a giant / beauty / small person: He / She stood at . . . feet, . . . inches (. . . meters), and . . . about . . . pounds (. . . kilos). He / She wore a (an) . . . and a (an) . . . and size . . . shoes / sneakers. Now that's a (an) . . . !

J. Dream wheels

The king rode in a magnificent armored truck and he provided a fine van for his body-guards. You can also have your dream motor vehicle! Use the words you know as well as those below to describe your dream car, truck, van, motorcycle, bus, or recreation vehicle.

Doors: two-door, four-door

Seats: two-person, five-person, nine-person . . .

Color: blue, red, white, green, black, metallic grey . . .

Options: armored, air-conditioned, remote-door opener, double cam, power-controlled windows, power-controlled locks, antilock brakes, global positioning maps, pre-accident sensors . . .

BEGIN LIKE THIS: My dream vehicle is a . . .

VOCABULARY

The King and I

Nouns

autofocus	door	island	people	shorts
bicycle	entrance	king	physician	size
bicycle touring	excitement	knee	policemen	smile
bodyguards	friend	letters	reply	sneaker
breakfast	gentleman	life	request	T-shirt
camera	giant	missionaries	resort	Tongan
chair	gym	motorcycles	rest periods	torso
Christian	gymnasium	office	sandals	truck
conversation	head	owner	secretary	van
country	interests	partner	shirt	village
doctor				

Adjectives

armored	earthly	heavenly	muscular	tall
baggy	friendly	lovely	personal	thin
beautiful	greatest	massive	several	white
brief	green	Mormon	short	young
confused				

Verbs

allow	click	learn	reply	tremble
answer	continue	leave	rest	visit
approach	escort	meet	ride	walk
arrange	exercise	mention	stand	wear
arrive	extend	notice	step out	weigh
ask	grant	open	take	whisper
assure	introduce	receive	think	zoom (in)
chat	kneel (down)			

Adverbs

already	comfortably	naturally	quickly	soon
closely	graciously	precisely	slowly	suddenly

Proper Nouns

Edwin	His Majesty	Royal Palace	Tongatapu
God the Father	Jim Hendrickson	South Pacific Ocean	United States
Good Samaritan Inn	King Taufa'ahau Tupou IV	Tonga	Western Samoa

Expressions

at first	I'll see what I can do.	to be pleased	to stay at
at last	I love it!	to my surprise	to take photographs
at the foot of	in the afternoon	to request an audience	to take pictures
by the way	Now that's a king!	to shake one's hand	to think to oneself
dressed in	to be eager	to spend a vacation	to set one's camera
How do you like . . . ?	to be honored		

6 Surprising Reykjavík

At first sight, Reykjavík, Iceland, is an Arctic town of colorful, boxy houses, gleaming° streets, and a salmon stream running through the center of the city. It's a great place. There's little crime, virtually no pollution (thanks to geothermal heat), 100 percent literacy, and some of the globe's most spectacular countryside.

bright

So why doesn't all the world travel at once to Reykjavík? Mostly because Icelandic immigration regulations° are very strict, and the job market is tight.° But it's worth visiting this fascinating Nordic city. Reykjavík seems like a place where every one of the city's inhabitants will show up° to help a beached° whale. It is also a city where eighteen-hour-long winter nights are celebrated by group swimming at dawn in one of the city's steamy geothermal pools.

rules
there are few jobs

come together / unable to swim

WHAT'S OUT THERE

The outdoors is so much a part of everyday life that Reykjavíkers have almost no sense of "recreation." Being outside is just part of being Icelandic. And why not? Within miles of Reykjavík you'll find fjords,° lava fields, hundreds of hot springs and geysers,° glacial rivers,° and colossal waterfalls.° Seals,° seabirds, and seventeen different species

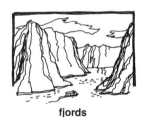

fjords

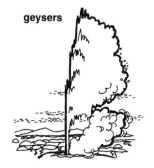

geysers

glacial rivers

hot springs

seals

of whales roam the coast. The nation's newest national park, three
hours north, holds the Snæfellsjökull glacier. Nordic and downhill skiing, snowboarding, sea kayaking, horseback riding, and any sport in-
volving ice are all standard workouts.° And for some of the finest fish-   forms of physical exercise
ing on the planet, you needn't leave downtown: Just pay your licensing
fee (about US $250) and cast° from your balcony into the Ellitaár.   throw out a fishing line

AROUND TOWN

During the workweek, this is a fairly bourgeois° city. Business ex-   middle class
ecutives, males and females, gather in the morning for a swim, then
head off° to downtown offices. At night, they read, then read some   go
more. Iceland publishes more books per capita° than any other nation.   per person
But then comes Thursday night, and the Icelandic weekend begins.
Hordes° of young people, clad° in this season's fashions, descend on   Many / dressed
the city's clubs and drink until the sun comes up—or in July, till it goes
down, which happens about 4 A.M.

LIVING QUARTERS

There are two types of housing in Reykjavík: modern and ubiq-
uitous° or wooden, older, and unavailable. Most of the downtown area   present everywhere
consists of square steel or concrete buildings softened with colorful paint
jobs. This is where young, cosmopolitan Reykjavíkers live, in sunny
two-bedroom apartments renting for about US $700 per month. Town-
homes nearby sell for US $150,000 or so. Graceful, pre–World War II
wooden cottages also dot the downtown areas but are much more rare
and therefore chic.° They cost at least US $175,000—if any are available.   fashionable

LEARNING ACTIVITIES

A. Check your comprehension

1. What is so "surprising" about Reykjavík, as indicated in the title of the reading?

2. For each category in the left-hand column, circle one word that best describes Reykjavík according to the reading.

a.	Climate	cool	warm	hot
b.	Pollution	low	average	high
c.	Jobs	few	some	many
d.	Crime	low	average	high

      e. **Literacy**   low   average   high

      f. **Sports**   few   some   many

      g. **Housing**   none   some   much

3. What sport would you most enjoy in Reykjavík? Why?

4. Would you like to visit that city? Why or why not?

5. Would you like to live in Reykjavík? Explain your reason(s).

B. Increasing your word power

1. Say whether the following actions can be done by people, animals, or both.

a. to run	**g.** to drink all night
b. to roam	**h.** to bathe in hot springs
c. to fish	**i.** to travel from place to place
d. to swim	**j.** to slide down a snow-covered mountain
e. to skate	**k.** to . . .
f. to show up	**l.** to . . .

2. **Word sets.** In each item below, cross out the word or expression that does not belong in the same category, and explain why it does not.

EXAMPLE: ~~dawn~~   season   winter   spring

        Dawn is not a season nor does it refer to a season.

a. cottages	hordes	townhouses	apartments
b. geysers	glaciers	fjords	whales
c. nation	globe	world	planet
d. seabirds	seals	females	whales
e. recreation	sea kayaking	horseback riding	snowboarding
f. streams	pools	waterfalls	species
g. lava fields	hot springs	geysers	glacial rivers

3. In English, the names of many leisure activities end in **-ing**. For each action verb below, name the activity or sport. In some cases, you can also indicate where the activity is done. If you wish, add names of activities you enjoy.

EXAMPLES: to sail a boat over an ocean → ocean sailing

to ski across the countryside → cross-country skiing

a. to drive   g. to watch whales

b. to skate   h. to take pictures *taking pictures*

c. to hunt   i. to hunt for a job *job hunting*

d. to snowboard   j. to swim with a group

e. to skateboard   k. to kayak in the sea

f. to ride a bike   l. to fish through a hole in the ice *ice fishing*

C. Comparing Reykjavík with my town and country

After reading the following sentences about Reykjavík, describe your hometown by finishing the incomplete sentences.

EXAMPLE: Osaka, Japan, is an *ancient* town.

1. Reykjavík, Iceland, is an Arctic town. It has boxy houses, gleaming streets, and a salmon stream in the center of town.

    _____, _____ is   a/an _____ town.   It   has
    (my town)   (my country)

    _____ houses, _____ streets, and a/an _____ in the center of town.

2. There are different types of housing in Reykjavík: two-bedroom apartments, modern townhouses, and wooden cottages. A two-bedroom apartment rents for about US $700 per month there. Older houses are usually unavailable.

    There   are   different   types   of   housing   in   _____: _____,
                                                          (my town)

    _____, and _____. A two-bedroom apartment rents for about US

    $_____ there. Older houses are _____.

3. In Reykjavík there's little crime, no pollution, and 100 percent literacy.

    In _____ there's _____ crime, _____ pollution, and
        (my town)

    _____ literacy.

4. In Iceland, immigration regulations are strict, and the job market is tight.

    In _____ immigration regulations are _____, and the job
        (my country)

    market is _____.

5. Within miles of Reykjavík visitors will find fjords, lava fields, and colossal waterfalls.

   Within miles of _____ visitors will find _____, _____,
                        (my town)
   and _____.

6. For some of the finest fishing on the planet, you needn't leave downtown Reykjavík: Just pay your licensing fee and cast from your balcony into the Ellitaár.

   For some of the finest _____ on the planet, you needn't leave
   _____. Just _____ and _____ in/at _____.
                            (action)   (action)   (place)

D. Speaking or writing project

Answer each of the following questions, either in small groups or in writing, according to your teacher's instructions.

Why do you suppose that . . .

1. Reykjavíkers read so much?
2. there are so few jobs in Reykjavík?
3. immigration regulations are very strict in Iceland?
4. few wooden cottages are available in Reykjavík?
5. so many young Reykjavíkers drink so much during summer?
6. ice-related sports are very popular in Iceland?
7. the sun goes down at about 4 A.M. in Reykjavík?

E. Fact and fantasy

1. Think about a city that you like very much, then answer the following questions:

   a. What is the name of the city you like so much?
   b. What country is it in, and where is it located (use a map)?
   c. Why do you like that city so much?
   d. How many people live there?
   e. What types of housing do they have?
   f. How do people earn a living there?
   g. What do they do in their free time?
   h. What is there to see and do outside the city?

2. Think about a city that you would like to visit one day if you had the time and money, then answer the following questions:

   a. What is the name of the city you would like to visit?

   b. What country is it in, and where is it located (use a map)?

   c. Why would you like to visit this city?

   d. Approximately how many people live there?

   e. What do they do for a living?

   f. What is there to see and do outside the city?

F. Land or sea?

The sea is very important to Iceland. Is the sea also important to your country? Read the following questions and discuss your responses with a classmate.

   1. Why is the sea important to your country?

   2. Why is the land important to your country?

   3. Which animals live near the coast? Which ones live in the forests, jungles, or deserts?

   4. What are some important activities that happen on the land and on the sea?

   5. Where have you lived for a long time? How long did you live there? What did you like best about that place? What did you like least?

   6. Would you prefer to live near the coast, beside a lake, or in the mountains? Why?

   7. Is the most developed region in your country the coast, the interior, the desert, or the mountains? Which area is *least* developed? Why?

G. The night is young

Night and day are very different concepts in an Arctic nation. In summer, Reykjavíkers can party until the 4 A.M. sunset. In winter, however, they have eighteen-hour nights and only six-hour-long days!

   1. Interview four students and find out what activities they would like to do during the summer and winter months in Reykjavík.

   2. Write down their answers, and add your own.

   3. Summarize the results of your informal survey and report back to the class.

   4. Determine which group of students was more original.

BEGIN LIKE THIS:

When the night is young, before the 4 A.M. sunset, many Reykjavíkers (want to . . . / would like to . . .) and also . . . Two of them would also like to . . . I would particularly enjoy . . . Eighteen hours of darkness is a very long time! I think I would . . . Most of my friends, however, would like to . . . Another idea is to . . .

H. Capturing Mother Nature's power

Geothermal energy is plentiful in Iceland, but sources of energy vary depending on geography and the geological composition of the earth in a given place. Describe sources of energy available in your country or area. Include all of them, even those that are not being used at present.

EXAMPLE: In my country / area there is . . . (geothermal / thermal / solar / hydraulic / wind) energy available. (Some / none) of that energy is used at present but I think we could build . . . If we had more _____ energy, pollution would be . . . I (don't) think this is possible because . . .

I. Having fun

Recreation and being outside are one and the same for Reykjavíkers. Is this true in your culture? Is recreation separate from other activities such as work and everyday chores? Describe your recreational activities for visitors to your country. At your teacher's request, also compare your activities with Reykjavíkers' activities.

BEGIN LIKE THIS:

Recreation is very important to us. On (Thursdays / Saturdays / Sundays) we all descend on . . . or we (visit relatives / go dancing / go drinking / dine out / go to the movies) . . .

VOCABULARY

Surprising Reykjavík

Nouns

apartments	females	job market	planet	sport
balcony	fjords	land	pollution	square steel
buildings	geysers	lava fields	pools	stream
business executives	glacier	licensing fee	recreation	swim
club	globe	life	regulations	swimming
coast	group	literacy	salmon	townhomes
concrete	heat	living quarters	sea kayaking	waterfalls
cottages	hordes	males	seabirds	weekend
countryside	horseback riding	nation	seals	whale
crime	hot springs	nights	season	winter
dawn	housing	offices	sense	workouts
downhill skiing	ice	outdoors	snowboarding	workweek
downtown	immigration	paint jobs	species	world
fashions	inhabitants	park		

Adjectives

Arctic	colorful	glacial	Nordic	sunny
available	colossal	gleaming	rare	surprising
beached	cosmopolitan	graceful	spectacular	tight
bourgeois	everyday	Icelandic	standard	ubiquitous
boxy	fascinating	modern	steamy	unavailable
chic	finest	national	strict	wooden
clad	geothermal	nearby		

Verbs

begin	descend	help	provide	sell
cast	dot	hold	publish	show up
celebrate	drink	involve	rent	soften
consist	gather	leave	roam	travel
cost	head off	pay	seem	

Adverbs

fairly	mostly	virtually

Proper Nouns

Ellitaár	Iceland	Reykjavík	Reykjavíkers	Snæfellsjökull

Expressions

at first sight	at once	per capita

Vocabulary Review
Unit III

A. Word sets

In each word set below, cross out the word that does *not* belong to it. Then explain why you crossed out the word in each set.

EXAMPLE: physician / policeman / ~~inhabitant~~ / bodyguard

An *inhabitant* is not a profession.

1. salmon / whales / seabirds / seals   _____

2. rare / colossal / massive / tall   _____

3. Tonga / Iceland / Reykjavík / Western Samoa   _____

4. at first / at home / at last / at once   _____

5. to whisper / to walk / to travel / to roam   _____

6. to click / to show up / to zoom in / to take pictures _____

7. snowboarding / horseback riding / downhill
   skiing / publishing   _____

B. Reading for meaning

Read the selection below. Then complete the reading with appropriate words and phrases from the following list.

smile, trucks, outdoors, young, night, surprise, began, like, sunny, fascinating, shook, dressed, love, sneakers, stayed, friendly, camera, United States

A Fascinating Adventure

When I was twenty years old, I was an adventurous _____ man. One day I _____ a _____ trip from my home in Wisconsin to Mexico. I left home in early June. I was _____ in jeans, T-shirt and _____. I carried a small backpack and an old _____ to take pictures along the way.

I hitchhiked across the _____ and into Mexico. Many _____ people gave me rides in their cars or _____. I always thanked them with a big _____ and _____ their hand. The weather was not always _____, but I still had a good time.

Sometimes I camped _____ and sometimes I _____ at small hotels. Several times people invited me to spend the _____ in their homes. To my _____, they asked me, "How do you _____ my town?" I usually answered, "I _____ it!"

C. Which do you prefer?

Mark or write in the blank *one* preference to complete each sentence below. Then read aloud your preferences to a classmate. Your teachers may ask you to say why you chose certain preferences.

1. I prefer to travel . . .
   _____ alone   _____ with a friend   _____

2. It's fun traveling with . . .
   _____ a male/female   _____ a friendly   _____
   partner   animal

3. When I travel abroad, I usually take a(an) . . .
   _____ camera   _____ bicycle   _____

4. I want to visit . . .
   _____ Iceland   _____ Tonga   _____

5. I prefer to visit . . .
   _____ small villages   _____ big cities   _____

6. I want to spend my next vacation in . . .
   _____ the South   _____ the North   _____
   Pacific   Atlantic

7. One day I'd like to see a(an) . . .
   _____ glacier   _____ fjord   _____

8. I like to travel . . .
   _____ by motorcycle   _____ by bicycle   _____

9. When I travel, I usually wear . . .
   _____ chic clothing   _____ beautiful jewelry   _____

10. I like taking pictures of . . .
    _____ colorful villages _____ friendly people   _____

D. Getting to know you

Ask a classmate the questions below. Write down his or her answers. When you finish, your classmate should ask you the same questions.

1. Would you like to take a trip around the world? If so, with whom would you go? Why? Where would you like to stop and visit? Why?

2. What means of transportation would you use? Airplane? Train? Car? Bus? Bicycle?

3. What sort of clothes would you take along (for example: T-shirts, sandals)?

4. What types of places would you like to visit (for example: hot springs, steamy jungles, lava fields)?

5. I will read aloud some adjectives. Tell me if they describe you. Say "Yes," "No," or "It depends" (and explain on what it depends).

chic	young	confused	friendly
strict	muscular	bourgeois	cosmopolitan
short			

E. Bon voyage!

Complete the crossword puzzle on the next page.

Bon voyage!

ACROSS

2. Middle-class
4. People who are paid to protect others
6. Give money for something
8. People who are sent abroad to spread religious beliefs
10. Present everywhere
11. A place to exercise
12. A large sea mammal
13. The center of a town
14. Talk

DOWN

1. Residents
3. Rules
5. Unusual or hard to find
7. Doctor
9. The opposite of "buy"
11. A very tall person

UNIT IV

HOME ENTERTAINMENT

7 A Language Lesson I Learned

To know another language, somebody once said, is to possess another soul.° That's the sort of talk that makes polyglots° feel great but scares those who've never learned a foreign language. The trouble with learning a new language is that it guarantees humiliation,° usually in a highly public way. My oldest friend once stormed° into a Venetian grocery and declared in Italian, "I believe in ham!" Another person I know, needing a napkin in a Québec ice-cream shop, got a big laugh by asking for "extra diapers"° in French. I myself have tried to purchase breasts in a barber shop, to no avail.°

The downside,° of course, is that the touristy expressions that are the lifeblood of phrasebooks become irrelevant° once you live abroad. Rarely, when you move to Istanbul or Oslo, will you have to say, "Excuse me, where is the hotel?" Instead, you'll need hard-core° phrases like "neck sprain,"° "Stop that noise!" and maybe even "Phillips-head screwdriver."° Remember: It is unacceptable to simply say these phrases really loudly or in a thick° accent. Locals never fall for° this, even when they know what you are saying.

The best way to learn a language is not a $2,000 week at Berlitz. (I tried that, and to this day the best I can do in Russian is proclaim, "The

spirit / people who speak
  many languages
embarrassment
ran quickly

without success
problem
not important

important
pain

hard-to-understand / believe

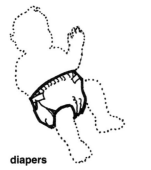

diapers

**Phillips-head
screw driver**

pen is red!") No, the ideal route is a far more slothful° and cheap enter-   lazy
prise. You must watch as much TV in your new country as you possibly
can. I know this from personal experience. As a kid,° thanks to my Ital-   child
ian grandparents, I could speak a respectable form of kitchen° Italian.   everyday
One step outside that sacred room, however, and I was struck dumb°—   couldn't speak
compelled to make strange, insectlike gestures to get my point across.
And most of my points,° in the end, seemed to involve soup or rice.   important details

    Years later, during an extensive stay in Rome, I had the opportu-
nity to watch months of Italian TV. Thanks to long spells° of mind-less   periods
gaping,° I could soon rattle on° like an auctioneer. The crucial tools in   watching TV / speak fluently
my mastery of the Italian language became (a) CNN broadcasts in Ital-
ian and (b) the European megastar known as Panto.

    Panto was an obese° fellow in a captain's outfit who presided over   fat
a game show that obliged contestants to remove items of clothing. The
overall effect was every bit as demeaning° as it sounds, but Panto boldly   embarrassing
persisted. (It's not me, his manner seemed to say. It's the game.) Thanks
to the endless banter° of Panto and his seminude guests, I acquired a   talking
wealth of useful slang. The wise expatriate° will not allow the wisdom   person who lives abroad
of Panto—of Pantos around the globe—to go to waste.° Because of the   to be lost
captain's on-screen endeavors, in no time I was dreaming in Italian.
That's always a sure sign that the language is seeping in.° Granted, given   being understood
Panto's role in my education, my dreams were at times disturbing.

    Good luck. Mind you,° once you become fluent in your new lan-   Listen
guage and start feeling superior to monolingual pals° back home, con-   friends
sider this: You'll never see an efficient post office or a decent grocery
store again. Not for the rest of your life.

LEARNING ACTIVITIES

A. Check your comprehension

How would the author of this reading answer the following questions?

1. The tone of my article is rather (funny / serious).
2. For me learning a foreign language is not (difficult / easy).
3. I think that it's (important / irrelevant) to learn the language of the country you are living in.
4. Speaking a foreign language clearly and with good pronunciation is (not very important / quite important) to the people you're speaking with.
5. Guidebooks (are / are not) very useful for people living abroad.
6. (Watching TV in the foreign language / Taking lessons at Berlitz) is the best way to learn another language.

7. (I took / I have never taken) formal lessons to learn another language.

8. I used to live in (Rome / Istanbul / Oslo / Québec / Moscow) where I learned to speak fluent (Turkish / Russian / French / Norwegian / Italian).

9. I remember a (comedian / sports announcer) whose name was Panto. By listening to him and his guests speak (German / Italian / Russian), I learned a lot of (sports terms / slang) in that language.

10. When you begin to (read / watch TV / dream) in a foreign language, you know that you're really learning it.

B. Increasing your word power

1. Study the following prefixes and their meaning.

PREFIXES	MEANING	SUFFIXES	MEANING
ex-	was once	**-able**	able, can
ir-	not	**-ful**	have much
mega-	big, important	**-less**	have none
poly-	many		

2. Complete the sentences below with appropriate words from the following list. Then complete the personalized questions with the appropriate information.

acceptable	expatriate(s)	megastar(s)	slothful
unacceptable	irrelevant	monolingual(s)	useful
respectable	relevant	polyglot(s)	useless

a. People who lived in the country in which they were born but now live abroad are _expatriates_.
   I was born in _____ and now I live in _____. Currently, (I
                     (country)   (country)
   am / I am not) an _____.

b. Well-known movie celebrities like Jodie Foster and Leonardo DiCaprio are international _megastars_.
   My favorite female _____ is _____. My favorite male
                                            (name)
   _____ is _____.
                      (name)

c. _monolinguals_ speak only one language, but _polyglots_ speaks two or more languages.
   I am a (_____) because I speak _____ languages: English,
                                              (number)
   _____ and _____.
    (language)   (language)

d. For me, using an English-language phrasebook is quite _useful_. It has

   many expressions and sentences that are _relevant_ to my needs.

  e. According to the author of the reading in this chapter, paying for expensive language lessons is a(an) _unacceptable_ way to learn. She feels it is more _acceptable_ to watch a lot of TV in the foreign language. I think that is _useful_ advice.

3. Say or write about what you do, using the adverbs below.

　　EXAMPLE:　outside:　After class my friends and I meet outside in a patio and talk.

abroad	highly	outside	possibly
always	later	rarely	simply
boldly	loudly	really	usually

C. Pat, English, and me

Complete the paragraphs below with appropriate words from the list.

at times	granted	good luck	to rattle on
in no time	I was struck dumb	thanks to	to get a laugh
in the end	back home	to get my point across	to this day
excuse me	fell for	to go to waste	to no avail
mind you			

　　At times, it's not easy to learn a foreign language. _Mind you_, it isn't that I don't study. I do! But _to this day_ English grammar sometimes confuses me.

　　Sometimes, _to get my point across_ to people, I use insectlike gestures. _Granted_, I look a bit odd doing that, but what else can I do? When people don't understand me, I say, "_Excuse me_," then I try to say it another way.

　　Once I bought a bilingual phrasebook to find certain expressions I wanted to say, but _to no avail_. The expressions just weren't in the phrasebook! I didn't want the book _to go to waste_, so I gave it to my niece as a present before she left for a trip to Canada.

　　Back home in Korea, my Australian friend Pat, helped me a lot with my English. _Thanks to_ her, I improved a lot. She used _to get a laugh_ out of the way I pronounced certain words, but _in the end_, she understood what I said.

　　Pat used _to rattle on_ about her family and friends in Sydney. One day _I was struck dumb_ when she told me that she was going to marry a man she had known for one week. Imagine that! She _fell for_ the guy in only one week!

　　Well, _in no time_ they were married. All I could tell my friend was, "_Good luck_, Pat!"

D. Great cities in our global village

Our global village has many great cities, including the twelve listed below. Complete the chart below, using a world atlas or an encyclopedia when necessary.

CITY	COUNTRY	CONTINENT	LANGUAGE	I VISITED	I WISH TO SEE
Atlanta	_____	_____	_____	☐	☐
Buenos Aires	_____	_____	_____	☐	☐
Istanbul	_____	_____	_____	☐	☐
Johannesburg	_____	_____	_____	☐	☐
Karachi	_____	_____	_____	☐	☐
Moscow	_____	_____	_____	☐	☐
New Delhi	_____	_____	_____	☐	☐
Osaka	_____	_____	_____	☐	☐
Québec	_____	_____	_____	☐	☐
Rome	_____	_____	_____	☐	☐
Sydney	_____	_____	_____	☐	☐
Tel Aviv	_____	_____	_____	☐	☐

E. People, places, and things

You probably know many different persons, places, and things. In the following list, write the name of a person, place, or thing.

a polyglot   _____

a foreign language   _____

my oldest friend   _____

an ice-cream shop   _____

a grocery store   _____

a little kid   _____

a sacred room   _____

a kind of soup   _____

a TV program   _____

a megastar   _____

a game show   _____

a monolingual pal   _____

F. My personal phrasebook

1. The author of the reading says that phrasebooks have limited use. No doubt, you have also used a phrasebook. For each situation below, write several useful phrases for a tourist or an expatriate.

   EXAMPLES:

   At a hotel reception desk: *"Excuse me, I have a reservation."*
   "What time is check out in the morning?"
   In a grocery store: *"How much are these bananas?"*
   "Can I pay with my Visa card?"

   a. In a barber shop
   b. In an ice-cream shop
   c. In a post office
   d. In a grocery store
   e. In a restaurant
   f. Speaking with a kid about his pals
   g. Not getting your point across to a local resident
   h. Being dumbstruck by a surprise birthday party
   i. Meeting a Russian student visiting your class
   j. Not understanding your teacher's slang expressions

2. Now sit with a classmate. Take turns reading aloud each situation and the phrases you wrote to accompany it. Your teacher may ask you to hand in your phrases when you have completed this speaking activity.

G. In my opinion

For each item below, read the opinion of the author who wrote the reading in this chapter. Afterward, express your own opinion by finishing the incomplete sentences. Either express your opinions to another student, or express them in writing, depending on your teacher's instructions.

1. "To know another language is to possess another soul."
   For me, knowing another language is important because . . .
2. "The trouble with learning a new language is that it guarantees humiliation."
   The biggest problem I have learning English is . . .
3. "Phrasebooks become irrelevant once you live abroad."
   I think that phrasebooks (are / are not) useful because . . .

4. "The best way to learn a language is to watch as much TV in your new country as possible."

   In my opinion, the best way to learn English is . . .

5. "The crucial tools in my mastery of Italian became CNN broadcasts and a game show."

   Two of my favorite English-language radio or television programs are . . .

6. "Dreaming is a sure sign that the foreign language is seeping in."

   Usually, I dream more in (my language / English) because . . .

H. Good advice

Only friends can speak frankly with friends. Using expressions from this chapter, write five pieces of advice for some of your friends and family members. The incomplete sentences below will help you.

EXAMPLES: Excuse me, Ali, but I think you should not miss so many classes.

1. Excuse me, but I think that you . . .
2. I have told you not to . . . , but to no avail. Why don't you . . . ?
3. If you don't stop . . . , you will . . .
4. Mind you, if you can . . . , you will never . . . again.
5. You will never have a decent . . . again if you don't stop . . .
6. If you don't . . . , you will not . . . Not for the rest . . .

I. Not for the rest of your life

Someone once said, "To know another language is to possess another soul."

1. Make a list of things that you would miss very much (if you lived abroad / now that you live abroad).

2. Write a paragraph explaining what things you miss and how much you miss them. To make your paragraph more interesting and original, use the expressions that you learned in this chapter.

   EXAMPLE: Mind you, I am very happy here but I really miss . . . Thanks to . . . , sometimes my friends and I eat / listen to / get together / talk about . . . Granted, it's not like being there but, excuse me, it is better than not eating / talking about . . . for the rest of your life. So, stop that . . . and let's . . . now.

J. Double humiliation

1. Form a group with two other students and make two lists of errors: (a) errors that you make when speaking English, and (b) common errors that foreigners make when speaking your language.

2. Read your lists to the class, explaining the errors, if necessary, and showing how to correct them. Your teacher can help you correct common errors in pronunciation and vocabulary.

3. At the end of the term, write and act out a funny situation using some of the errors you have collected and the expressions learned in this chapter (see the vocabulary list below). You will learn how humiliation and a thick accent can be fun!

VOCABULARY

A Language Lesson I Learned

Nouns

accent	endeavors	ham	napkin	room
auctioneer	enterprise	hotel	neck sprain	route
banter	expatriate	humiliation	noise	sign
barber shop	experience	ice-cream shop	opportunity	slang
breasts	expressions	items	outfit	soul
broadcasts	fellow	kid	pals	soup
captain	form	kitchen Italian	Phillips-head screwdriver	spells
clothing	game show	language	phrasebooks	stay
contestants	gaping	lesson	phrases	step
country	gestures	lifeblood	points	tools
diapers	globe	locals	polyglots	trouble
downside	grandparents	manner	post office	wealth
dreams	grocery	mastery	rice	wisdom
education	grocery store	megastar	role	years
effect	guests			

Adjectives

Berlitz	demeaning	extensive	ideal	mindless
cheap	disturbing	extra	insectlike	monolingual
compelled	efficient	fluent	irrelevant	obese
crucial	endless	foreign	Italian	oldest
decent	European	hard-core	long	on-screen

overall	Russian	strange	thick	useful
personal	sacred	superior	touristy	Venetian
public	seminude	sure	unacceptable	wise
respectable	slothful			

Verbs

acquire	dream	move	proclaim	seem
allow	feel	need	purchase	seep in
become	guarantee	oblige	remember	sound
believe	involve	persist	remove	storm
consider	know	possess	scare	watch
declare	learn	preside over		

Adverbs

abroad	highly	outside	really	simply
always	later	rarely	possibly	usually
boldly	loudly			

Proper Nouns

| Istanbul | Oslo | Panto | Québec | Rome |

Expressions

at times	granted	thanks to	to get a laugh	to no avail
back home	in no time	to be struck dumb	to get my point across	to rattle on
excuse me	in the end	to fall for	to go to waste	to this day
good luck	mind you			

8 Hooked on[1] <u>Telenovelas</u>

[1] *Hooked on* means addicted to.

In 1992, as the former nation of Yugoslavia tore itself apart in a frenzy° of ethnic slaughter, a far sweeter note played on television. A Mexican *telenovela*—or soap opera—known as *Los Ricos También Lloran* ("The Rich Cry Too") aired in the warring republics. Starring Verónica Castro, the diva° of *telenovelas*, it was the story of Mariana, a poor girl, maid to a rich family, who falls in love with the family's son, has his child, is rejected by him, must give up her child, and so on until the happy ending. Every night while it played in Serbia and Croatia, where at the time happy endings were at a premium,° life would stop for an hour.

    Kasia Wyberko, Balkan correspondent for Televisa, the network that produced *Los Ricos*, remembers rapt° crowds gathered in front of department store televisions.

    "I traveled a lot between the two countries," says Wyberko. The reaction was the same in Belgrade, Serbia, as it was in Zagreb, Croatia. The streets were totally empty. For a moment, this Mexican *telenovela* united two peoples at war.

    It was also the highest-rated° show on Croatian television. Since then, Mexican *telenovelas* have swept the world up in their teary melodramas° of romance, passion, good and evil, betrayal,° lies, and happy endings.

    Televisa, Mexico's massive entertainment system, is the world's largest producer of *telenovelas*. It now sells them throughout Latin America, as well as to 125 other countries. China has aired twenty-two Mexican *telenovelas.* Three Televisa *telenovelas* compete during prime time° every night on Indonesia's three main stations. The network's newest *telenovela* sensation, Thalia, was mobbed° both times she visited the Philippines in the last year. *Cuna de Lobos* ("Den of Wolves") was a huge hit in Australia. Amazingly, Televisa now claims its *telenovelas* are Mexico's largest export product.

rage

famous actress

rare

very interested

most popular

very sad dramas / cheating

the most popular viewing time / crowded with people

Other eras had Grimm's fairy tales or the stories of Dickens and Balzac. Today the Mexican *telenovela* is the fable° for our high-tech global village. It offers romance that begins, falters, blooms, falters again, and finally succeeds in 160 half-hour episodes. If ratings dip,° a hasty ending is improvised.°

    story
    go down
    invented

The *telenovela* is produced with international success and, some say, with far more creativity in Brazil and Venezuela, as well. But Mexico—which is to say Televisa—made it the enormous global business it is today. The company has produced more than two thousand *telenovelas* and creates twenty-two new series each year.

The thirty-nine-year-old genre has become Mexico's great cultural sponge—supplanting° cinema and theater. It absorbs actors, writers, and directors who find other genres increasingly hard to find. "If you want to promote a singer, put her in a *telenovela*," says Alvaro Cueva, a *telenovela* author. "In Mexico, everything converges° in the *telenovela*."

    replacing

    comes together

Until recently, the *telenovela* was the domain of the poor, watched by maids and working-class housewives. In 1977, *Simplemente María*—about a poor woman who through hard work becomes a successful fashion designer—caused a run° on sewing machines. *Dallas* and *Dynasty* aired in Mexico in the 1980s and convinced producers to improve the quality of *telenovelas*. International sales have continued that trend.

    rush to buy

Still, the *telenovela* continues to live with the scorn° of Latin American artists and intellectuals. Even the middle class is loathe° to admit watching them. "My students hang° their heads when they tell me they've found work in the *telenovelas*," says Alfredo Troncoso, a communications professor at the New World University outside Mexico City.

    hate
    ashamed
    lower

The classic *telenovela* plot° is the Cinderella story: Poor but virtuous° girl, usually a maid, falls in love with rich young man. Bad relatives try to separate them, and she suffers. Finally a rich and childless old man proves to be the maid's long-lost uncle. Lovers marry and live happily ever after. In that way, the *telenovela* differs from American soap operas. Currently, eight *telenovelas* show every night at prime time in Mexico, a sure sign that the genre now appeals to a broad class of people.

    storyline
    good

The world has become middle-class in its tastes if not its pocketbook.° Laura Castellot, who wrote a book about the history of Mexican television, agrees. "What's the dream everyone has? Let's call it American *modus vivendi:*° to have a car, a house, comforts," she says. "The dream is the same everywhere."

    wallet

    way of life

And, strangely, it is the Mexican *telenovela* that now best articulates° that American dream around the world.

    expresses

LEARNING ACTIVITIES

A. Check your comprehension

Match the columns below according to the information in the reading.

1. __d__ Televisa
2. __g__ Cinderella
3. __h__ Telenovelas
4. __b__ Warring republics
5. __a__ An old soap opera
6. __e__ The American dream
7. __c__ Venezuela and Brazil
8. __f__ Grimm, Dickens, Balzac

a. *Simplemente María*
b. Croatia and Serbia
c. Produce the best telenovelas
d. Produces Mexican telenovelas
e. Having many material comforts
f. Wrote famous stories in Europe
g. Has a classic telenovela plot
h. Mexico's largest export product

Answer the following items according to the reading selection.

1. To how many countries does Televisa export telenovelas? *125*
2. Name six countries where Mexican telenovelas are popular.
3. Name a popular soap opera from . . .
   a. the 1970s *Simplemente María*
   b. the 1980s *Dallas + Dynasty*
   c. the 1990s *Los Ricos... Italia...*
4. Why are Mexican soap operas so popular in our global village? *represent the Amer. Dream*

B. Increasing your word power

1. Match the words or expressions in the left-hand column with their meanings in the right-hand column. Use the reading selection in this chapter to help you.

__c__ eras
__a__ genres
__d__ to air
__f__ to star
__g__ ratings
__e__ rejection

a. Kinds of movies or books
b. Sad stories of human drama
c. Important or historical time periods
d. To transmit a television program
e. No longer paying attention to a former friend or lover
f. To play the main role in a movie or theatrical production

_____ melodramas   **g.** Percentages of how well or poorly viewers liked a program

_____ prime time   **h.** Time when many people are watching television at the same time

2. Group the useful verb phrases below into the three categories given.

to air a telenovela / to be at a premium / to be mobbed by people / to become famous / to dip in ratings / to fall in love / to give up one's child / to act in a movie / to star in a movie / to tear oneself apart

   a. Relating to television and acting

   b. Evoking negative ideas or feelings

   c. Evoking positive ideas or feelings

C. A Cinderella story

Complete the fairy tale below by using appropriate phrases and expressions from the list. You may use a phrase or expression more than once, providing that you use it appropriately.

in time	once upon a time	fall in love	at a premium
one day	happily ever after	fell in love	nevertheless
for a moment	give up	swept María off her feet	modus vivendi
in those days	hooked on	by chance	

Once upon a time a young maid named María worked for a rich family in Mexico City. The family had a handsome son, Carlos, who was the same age as María. _In those days_ young, handsome men were truly _at a premium_. _Indeed_, María _fell in love_ with Carlos and, _for a moment_, she thought he loved her. She was truly _hooked on_ the fellow, but there was one problem: María was poor. _Nevertheless_, she could not _give up_ the idea of marrying Carlos. Whenever she looked at his handsome face, she sighed and said silently to herself: "I love you, my darling."

One day Carlos took advantage of his young maid's love for him, and _in time_ María gave birth to their son, whom she named Miguelito. But Carlos rejected both María and Miguelito; he wanted nothing to do with them. Cruelty seemed to be the young man's _modus vivendi_.

By chance, Carlos had an uncle, Pablo, who was sixty years old, rich, balding, and single. The childless Pablo had always wanted a family, and he took pity on María and her baby. Soon Pablo _fell in love_ with María. And María began to _fall in love_ with Pablo.

One day Pablo _swept María off her feet_: he asked her to marry him. Without hesitation, the young maid accepted his proposal. And so it was that the couple married and moved with little Miguelito to a mountain village far from Mexico City and lived ___happily ever after___.

D. Are you a couch potato?

A "couch potato" is a person who watches a lot of television. Are you a couch potato? First, complete this activity in writing. Then tell a classmate the kinds of TV programs you watch and don't watch, how frequently (almost never, sometimes, almost always), and why.

EXAMPLE: international news
           I almost always watch the international news because I want to know what's happening in the world.

Almost never = 1   Sometimes = 2   Almost always = 3

Kinds of TV Programs

_____ local news		_____ game shows
_____ old movies		_____ soap operas
_____ sports programs		_____ talk shows
_____ international news		_____ documentaries
_____ programs in English		_____ weather forecasts

Now be more specific.

One of my favorite TV programs is "_____" because . . . A program that I want to see again is called "_____." I think that it's a very _____ program because . . . A television program that I don't recommend watching is called "_____." I don't like it because . . .

E. Interview

Ask a classmate the following questions.

1. How many TV sets do you have at home? In which rooms are they located?
2. How often do you watch television? Which days do you watch TV the most? The least? Why?
3. What's your favorite TV program? Why do you like it so much?
4. What are some benefits of watching TV? What are some negative aspects of watching television?

As a follow-up activity, write your answers to the questions above as a homework assignment.

F. Film classics

The list below gives the titles of some classic films that were produced in the United States. Indicate the type of film it is, as in the following example.

EXAMPLE: *Close Encounters of the Third Kind*
           science fiction

FILM TITLE   FILM TYPE

1. *Airplane*   action
2. *Toy Story*   drama
3. *Sherlock Holmes*   comedy
4. *Laurel and Hardy*   cartoon
5. *Gone with the Wind*   Western
6. *How the West Was Won*   mystery
7. *ET: The Extraterrestrial*   science fiction

G. Let's go to the movies!

Ask a classmate the following questions.

1. How often do you go to the movies?
2. When do you usually go to the movies? Whom do you go with?
3. What's the name of one of your favorite movies? Why do you like it so much? When did you see it? What was the movie about?
4. Who's your favorite actor and actress? Why?
5. Would you like to be an actor / actress? Why or why not?
6. Would you like to be a film producer or director? Why or why not?
7. Some movie stars earn a lot of money, but what do they lose?

H. Improve your writing skills

1. *Associations:* Study the meaning of adjective-noun pairs in the list below. For each pair, write an example from the reading or provide an example from your own experience. Use the phrases in sentences.

   EXAMPLE: warring republics
              Serbia and Croatia were warring republics.

poor girl	hasty ending	warring republics	rejected lover
prime time	sweet note	American lifestyle	highly-rated show
happy ending	American dream	rapt TV viewers	international sales

| hard work | ethnic slaughter | cultural sponge | middle-class taste |
| teary melodramas | | | global business |

2. *Expansions:* In English, it is possible to place two or more nouns together. First, study the meaning of the noun phrases below. Second, write four or five noun phrases that you know. Your teacher may also ask you to use the noun phrases in sentences.

EXAMPLE: color television sets
         department store furniture

soap opera	makeup artist	screen writer	television producer
cable TV	CNN interview	movie director	telenovela author
TV channel	TV network	fashion designer	entertainment system

I. Lights, camera, action!

1. Work with two or three classmates. Write a brief TV program entitled *Today's News* or *Tomorrow's Weather.* Follow these steps:

   a. Collect the necessary information that you need to write your program.

   b. Organize this information in a logical form.

   c. Write the most important ideas about this information in two or three short paragraphs.

   d. Exchange your paragraphs with students in another group, and correct any errors you find.

   e. Rewrite your paragraphs, then hand them in to your teacher for correction.

   f. Write the final version of your TV program.

2. Present your TV program to the class. If possible, film the program with a videocamera to view it afterward.

VOCABULARY

Hooked on Telenovelas

Nouns

actors	business	comforts	creativity	diva
artists	car	communications	crowds	domain
author	child	company	den	dream
betrayal	cinema	correspondent	department store	ending
book	class	countries	directors	entertainment system

episodes
eras
evil
export product
fable
fairy tales
family
fashion designer
frenzy
genre
girl
global
heads
history
hit
hour

house
housewives
intellectuals
lies
life
lovers
maid
man
melodramas
(the) middle class
nation
network
night
note
passion
people

peoples
plot
pocketbook
(the) poor
prime time
producer
professor
quality
ratings
reaction
relatives
republics
romance
sales
scorn
sensation

series
sewing machines
show
sign
singer
slaughter
soap opera
son
sponge
station
story
stories
streets
students
success

tastes
telenovelas
television
theater
time
trend
uncle
village
wolves
woman
work
(the) working class
world
writers
year

Adjectives

American
bad
Balkan
best
broad
childless
classic
Croatian
cultural

empty
enormous
ethnic
former
global
great
half-hour
happy
hard

hasty
highest-rated
high-tech
huge
international
largest
last
Latin American
loath

long-lost
main
massive
Mexican
newest
old
poor
rapt
rejected

rich
successful
sure
sweeter
teary
virtuous
warring
young

Verbs

absorb
admit
agree
air
appeal
articulate
become
begin
bloom
call
cause

claim
compete
continue
converge
convince
create
differ
dip
falter
find

hang
have
improve
improvise
live
marry
mob
offer
produce
promote

prove
put
remember
scheme
sell
separate
show
star
stop
succeed

suffer
supplant
tear apart
tell
travel
unite
visit
want
watch
write

Adverbs

amazingly	increasingly	outside	still	totally
currently	interminably	recently	strangely	usually
finally				

Proper Nouns

Alfredo Troncoso	China	Kasia Wyberko	Mexico	Televisa
Alvaro Cueva	Cinderella	Latin America	Mexico City	Venezuela
Australia	Croatia	Laura Castellot	New World University	Verónica Castro
Balzac	Dickens	María	Philippines	Yugoslavia
Belgrade	Grimm	Mariana	Serbia	Zagreb
Brazil	Indonesia			

Expressions

a run on	at war	hooked on	to fall in love	to sweep the world up
and so on	for a moment	in that way	to give up	which is to say
at a premium	happily ever after	*modus vivendi*		

Vocabulary Review
Unit IV

A. Word sets

In each word set below, cross out the word that does *not* belong to it. Then explain why you crossed out the word in each set.

EXAMPLE: huge / ~~wise~~ / massive / large

The adjective *wise* does not refer to size.

1. ham / soup / rice / den   _____
2. pal / diva / accent / kid   _____
3. loath / evil / trouble / decent   _____
4. Venetian / Russian / Croatian / Mexican   _____
5. world / global / international / ethnic   _____
6. Yugoslavia / Venezuela / Mariana / Indonesia   _____
7. auctioneer / expatriate / captain / maid / producer   _____
8. grocery / enterprise / department store / ice-cream shop   _____

B. Reading for meaning

Read the selection below. Then complete the reading with appropriate words and phrases from the following list.

hooked, outside, going to waste, watch, television, still, grandparents, prime time, remember, rattle, screen, hard-core, high-tech, enormous, scorn, dream, pals, at times, given up, megastars, classic, cinema, become

Hooked on Television

When I was ten years old, my family had one of the first _____ sets in our neighborhood. I _____ that it had a ten-inch _____ that was built into an _____ wooden cabinet.

Every Saturday all my _____ would visit me, not to play outside but to watch _____ Western movies with _____ like Roy Rogers and Gene Autry. Soon we became _____ on Westerns and, within several months, we were _____ TV viewers. In fact, I used to _____ so many cowboy movies on television and at the _____, that I began to _____ I had a horse and a pistol, and lived in the Old West.

On Sundays my _____ visited my family. _____, they would look at me with _____ when I was watching television. They didn't like _____ entertainment systems at all. My grandmother used to tell me, "Go _____ play with your friends or ride your bicycle." Then she would _____ on about how my childhood was _____ and how I was going to _____ blind by watching so much TV.

My grandparents are dead now and many of my childhood friends are grandparents themselves. Apart from working and visiting my friends, I _____ have time to watch an occasional documentary movie during _____. And I have not _____ my love for old Westerns.

C. Which do you prefer?

Mark or write in the blank *one* preference to complete each sentence below. Then read aloud your preferences to a classmate.

1. For me, TV ratings are . . .

    _____ important   _____ unimportant   _____

2. I prefer to watch . . .

    _____ soap operas   _____ game shows   _____

3. I can easily give up . . .

    _____ watching TV   _____ listening to music _____

4. Someday I want to meet a famous . . .

    _____ director   _____ actor   _____

5. I would like an opportunity to become . . .

    _____ famous   _____ successful   _____

6. I enjoy reading . . .

    _____ fashion magazines _____ European newspapers _____

7. I also like reading . . .

    _____ fairy tales   _____ romances   _____

8. I like stories that are . . .

    _____ melodramatic   _____ classic   _____

9. I read in English . . .

    _____ to become fluent _____ to increase my vocabulary _____

10. I also learn lots of English slang by . . .

    _____ watching TV   _____ listening to the radio _____

D. Getting to know you

Ask a classmate the questions below. Write down his or her answers. When you finish, your classmate should ask *you* the questions. Your teacher may ask you to explain why you chose certain preferences.

1. In your country, what do middle-class people do to have fun at home?

2. How do *you* entertain yourself at home?

3. How many hours do you watch TV every day? What is your favorite TV program? Why do you like it so much?

4. I will read a list of home entertainment items. Say "Yes" if you have the item or "No" if you do not have it.

computer	tape recorder	television set	VCR
pool table	CD-ROM player	playing cards	ping pong table
stereo radio			

5. I will read aloud some adjectives. Tell me if they describe you. Say "Yes," "No," or "It depends" (and explain on what it depends).

wise	efficient	respectable	virtuous
decent	successful	European	childless
Mexican			

E. Home entertainment

Complete the crossword puzzle on the next page.

Home entertainment

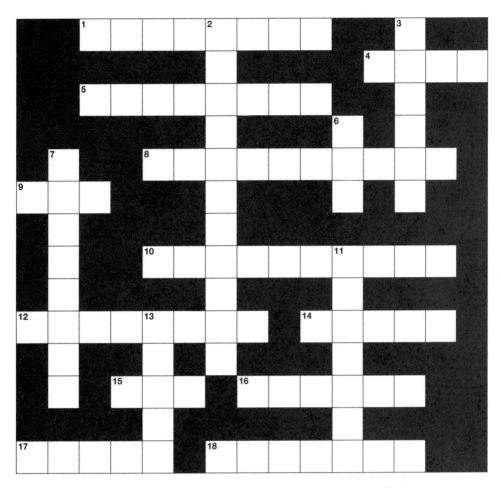

ACROSS

1. Lazy
4. Friends, especially among children
5. Very large
8. Dramatic plays
9. Another word for a successful movie or drama
10. Another word for business
12. A person who speaks more than one language
14. The opposite of full
15. Not the truth
16. Rage
17. What people do when
18. To own

DOWN

2. Embarrassment
3. A French author of the nineteenth century
6. Another word for automobile
7. Very good, especially when referring to personality
11. A romantic novel
13. A nineteenth-century German writer of fables

UNIT V

HUMAN LIFE SCIENCES

9 Cloning: Duplicating[1] Human Beings

---

[1]*Duplicating* means making copies.

Can you imagine a world in which hundreds, thousands, or millions of people look alike?° They have the same face, the same eye and hair color, and the same height. In short,° they are replicas° of one person. This world of people who look like each other° may be possible soon.

resemble each other
In a few words / copies
the same

Traditionally, all human life begins with the union of a sperm (male cell) and an egg (female cell). But we know now that every cell in a person's body contains genetic° information. If a body cell could divide and grow, therefore, the result could be a replica of the donor.° This method of reproduction is called "cloning." Cloning works° with humans, plants, insects, and animals.

referring to genes
person who gave the cell
can be done

In 1968, Dr. J. B. Gurdon of Oxford University in England, took an unfertilized egg from a frog.° He destroyed° the egg's nucleus and its genetic information. Then he took a *body* cell from a different frog and put its nucleus into the egg cell. The new tadpole° was the exact copy of the "donor" frog.

tadpole

killed

Could this method of reproduction work with humans in the future? It may be possible. First, doctors would take a healthy egg from a woman and destroy the nucleus. Then a nucleus from another person's body cell would replace the destroyed nucleus. The egg would be put into the uterus° of a woman where it would grow into a replica of the donor. Because every person has trillions of body cells that he or she can donate, the process of reproduction could be repeated many times.

frog

organ where a baby
grows before birth

What would a world of cloned humans be like?° First of all, the family would not exist as we know it; the ideas of "mother" and "father" would be different. Also, political leaders could order doctors to clone millions of soldiers—all of them looking alike. People could reproduce many clones of themselves and they could find a new form of immortality!°

resemble, look like

living forever

Today, some doctors fertilize human eggs artificially in test tubes°
in medical laboratories. Then they implant° the fertilized eggs in hu-   put
man mothers. The results are called "test-tube babies." If people accept
cloning as they have accepted artificial fertilization, human society will
change—perhaps beyond recognition.

test tubes

LEARNING ACTIVITIES

A. Check your comprehension

Decide if each statement below is true or false according to the reading selection. If the
statement is false, say why.

F   **1.** Human clones are possible today.

F   **2.** Most plants and animals can be cloned.

T   **3.** It is now possible to clone frogs.

F   **4.** Tadpoles develop into fish.

T   **5.** Doctors can produce test-tube babies.

F   **6.** Cloning will help people live longer.

T   **7.** Cloning will probably change our world.

F   **8.** Doctors produce test-tube babies and clones in the same way.

T   **9.** The union of a male with a female cell results in a fertilized egg.

F   **10.** Scientists make clones by putting one body cell into another body cell.

B. Say it aloud!

Repeat the following words and phrases after your teacher.

1. Fertilization and reproduction

Sex Cells

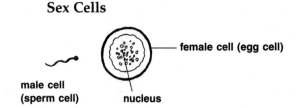

male cell
(sperm cell)   nucleus

female cell (egg cell)

2. Cloning

Replicas: $\Big\langle$ look alike

look like each other

3. *-tion*

information, tradition, recognition, fertilization, reproduction

4. *-al*

medical ⟶ medical technology
artificial ⟶ artificial fertilization
political ⟶ political leaders

5. final *-s*

humans ⟶ millions of humans
plants $\Big\}$ billions of plants and animals
animals

6. insects   trillions of insects

to divide ⟶ dividing ⟶ divided ⟶ undivided
to fertilize ⟶ fertilizing ⟶ fertilized ⟶ unfertilized
to duplicate ⟶ duplicating ⟶ duplicated ⟶ unduplicated

C. Word families

Verbs, nouns, and adjectives often form word families.

EXAMPLE: to differ, difference, different

1. Complete the chart of word families. Consult the reading or use your dictionary when necessary.

VERBS	NOUNS	ADJECTIVES
to reproduce	reproduction	reproductive
to _clone_	clone, cloning	_cloned_
to _destroy_	destruction	destructive, destroyed
to _inform_	_information_	informative
to _accept_	acceptance	acceptable
to donate	_donation_	_donated_
to grow	_growth_	grown
to _know_	knowledge	knowledgeable

2. Complete the paragraphs. Use the words from the word family chart in (1).

Someday it may be possible to ___clone___ a human being. People will ___donate___ their body cells just like blood donors.

But many people cannot ___accept___ the idea of cloning a human being. They think that this method of ___reproduction___ will destroy human society as we ___know___ it.

We need more ___knowledge___ about cloning. We need to ___know___ how it will change the way we live and think. The rapid ___growth___ of technology is changing our lives every day. Some people think that technology is ___destructive___, but others think that it is good for our society.

D. Hello, Dolly!

In the 1990s, scientists cloned a sheep, which they named "Dolly." Learn about Dolly's story by completing the following paragraph with appropriate words from the list.

cloned	replaced	copy	uterus
cloning	egg	Dolly	

Dolly, a two-year old sheep living in England, is a world celebrity. She is a clone or the exact ___copy___ of another sheep. A group of scientists interested in ___cloning___ took several eggs from a sheep to produce the first ___cloned___ sheep. First, they ___replaced___ the nucleus of each egg with nuclei taken from the body cells of another sheep. Then they implanted the egg with a new nucleus in the mother sheep. This was the most difficult part: to get the new ___egg___ to live in a sheep's ___uterus___. Finally, the scientists were successful. Several months later, ___Dolly___ was born. Dolly was the first cloned mammal in the world!

E. Crossword puzzle

Complete the crossword puzzle on the opposite page. Most of the words are from the reading.

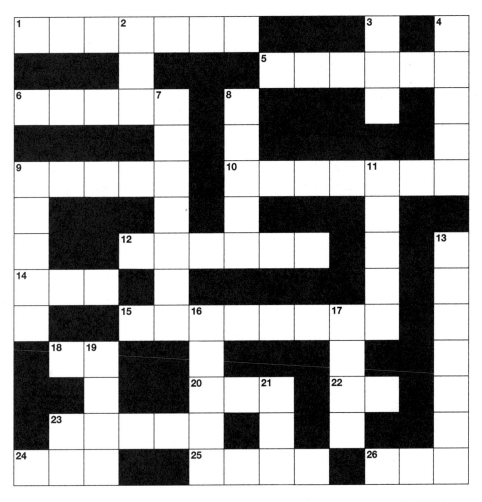

ACROSS

1. Another word for "maybe"
5. Opposite of "father"
6. Opposite of "last"
9. The _____ is our global village
10. Animals such as flies and spiders
12. Person who works in a hospital
14. You _____ me. (conjunction)
15. "_____-_____" babies began in a lab
18. United States _____ America
20. The female cell
22. Please _____ on time, Craig.
23. Person who gives blood
24. Animal that barks
25. Opposite of "few"
26. Past tense of "am"

DOWN

2. I have; he _____
3. Definite article
4. I grow; the cell _____
7. An animal that becomes a frog
8. to be
9. a female person
11. A live replica of a plant, animal, or human being
13. The central part of a living cell
16. The male cell
17. A new human being
19. A green animal that jumps and lives near water
21. Another word for "pistol"
23. Another word for "make"

F. Can and could

You read that scientists can and cannot do certain things today. Ten or twenty years ago they could do some things but they could not do other things. Practice using *can* and *could,* and their negative forms by completing each sentence.

1. a. _____ you divide 32 by 4? Of course, I _____ .

   b. _____ you multiply 224 by 18? No, I _____. I need my calculator to do that.

   c. _____ you make bread? No, but my mother _____ .

   d. _____ you donate blood? No, I _____ because I have a cold.

   e. When you were ten years old, _____ you play soccer well? Yes, I _____ , but my little brother _____n't.

2. a. Scientists _____ clone human beings yet.

   b. Twins _____ come either from the same egg or from two different eggs.

   c. Albert Einstein was a famous scientist who _____ fill out his income tax forms correctly. Isn't that strange?

   d. Genes contain genetic information. Genes _____ also transmit some diseases.

   e. In some countries, women _____ get an abortion. In other countries an abortion _____ be performed without legal problems.

   f. Today, scientists _____ clone frogs, but only twenty years ago they _____ .

3. a. Twenty years ago in my country, people could / couldn't . . .

   Today they can / still can't . . .

   b. Last year I could / couldn't . . .

   This year I can / still can't . . .

G. What do you think?

People have different opinions about cloning. What is your opinion? Read each sentence below. Then put an X on the scale to express your opinion.

1. In the future only clones will live in some communities.

   |_____|_____|_____|_____|_____|
   impossible   maybe   possible

2. All human cells have the information for cloning a new person.

   |_____|_____|_____|_____|_____|
   uncertain   maybe   certain

3. Sex cells are necessary for human reproduction.

|_____|_____|_____|_____|_____|
uncertain   maybe   certain

4. Any body cell can divide and grow.

|_____|_____|_____|_____|_____|
impossible   maybe   possible

5. Without a donor's nucleus, doctors cannot reproduce a clone.

|_____|_____|_____|_____|_____|
uncertain   maybe   certain

6. Scientists can make living replicas of themselves in a lab.

|_____|_____|_____|_____|_____|
improbable   maybe   probable

7. If doctors clone humans beings, they will need women to help.

|_____|_____|_____|_____|_____|
uncertain   maybe   certain

8. Cloning will destroy human society as we know it today.

|_____|_____|_____|_____|_____|
uncertain   maybe   certain

H. Cloning and you

1. Imagine that you are an important political leader in your country. You have the power to order doctors to clone anything and anyone. Who would you want to clone? Why? How many clones would you want? Why?

2. If you could create the ideal person, what would he or she be like?

EXAMPLES: He would have Einstein's intelligence.
                    She would have Hillary Clinton's energy.

_____ courage   _____ personality   _____ body
_____ voice   _____ charm   _____ sense of humor
_____ face   _____ intelligence   __?__ _____?_____
_____ energy

3. Which parts or characteristics of your body or personality (face, intelligence, cheerfulness, etc.) would you like your children to have?

4. Suppose you donate a cell from your body to make a clone.

   a. Would the baby clone be your son or daughter, or your brother or sister?
   b. Who would take care of the baby?
   c. If you died, would the baby receive your money and other things that you have?

I. Color game

1. Work with a conversation partner. Say if you agree or disagree with each statement below, then say why. You can begin your answer like this:

   EXAMPLE: Human cloning is good for our world.
   Agreement: Human cloning is a good idea because . . .
   Disagreement: Human cloning is not a good idea because . . .

   a. Human cloning is good for our world.
   b. I would like a clone of myself.
   c. Making human clones will destroy families.
   d. It is all right to clone plants and animals but not people.
   e. Cloning human beings should be illegal in every country.
   f. It is okay to clone very intelligent or creative people.
   g. People should accept human cloning as part of the progress of science.
   h. Cloning specific cells is fine to make livers and kidneys available for transplants.

2. Your teacher may ask you to write your opinions to the statements in (1) above. If so, you can begin your answers like this:

   EXAMPLE: Cloning is good for our world.
   Agreement: Human cloning is good for our world because . . .
   Disagreement: I disagree. In my opinion, human cloning is . . .

VOCABULARY

Cloning: Duplicating Human Beings

Nouns

cell	frog	laboratory	society	result
cloning	height	leader	soldier	tadpole
copy	idea	method	sperm	test-tube (baby)
doctor	immortality	nucleus	recognition	union
donor	information	plants	replica	uterus
egg	insects	process	reproduction	woman
fertilization				

Adjectives

artificial	exact	healthy	medical	trillion
cloned	female	human	political	unfertilized
destroyed	genetic	male	possible	

Verbs

clone	divide	fertilize	imagine	repeat
contain	donate	find	implant	replace
destroy	exist	grow	order	reproduce

Adverbs

artificially	soon	today	traditionally

Proper Nouns

England   Oxford University

Expressions

first of all	in short	therefore	to look alike	to look like

Jeanne Calment, 122 years old

10 Extending the Human Life Span[1]

[1]*Life span* means length of life.

Whon Jeanne Calment of Arles, France, died in August 1997, the world paid attention. She was not an actress, politician, or other famous person, but that didn't matter.° What caught the public's attention was Calment's unusually° long life. At 122, she was probably the world's oldest person.

°was not important
°more than normal

Can others expect to live as long as Calment, or perhaps even longer? After all, the human life span has increased slowly in the twentieth century. Will this trend continue? What is the maximum age that human beings will live? Researchers in different fields are exploring° these questions, with some exciting possibilities.

°investigating

- At Hong Kong University of Science and Technology, researchers are investigating ways that free radicals° protect human tissue.° They are especially interested in how traditional Chinese medicines slow the aging process.° Many of these medicines come from herbs and other organic materials.

°chemical elements / group of cells with common function
°the way people get older

- At the University of Sussex, England, scientists are trying to isolate° genes that affect how long humans live. Of special interest is the role of the telomere, a section at the end of chromosomes° that grows shorter with age.

°separate
°part of a cell's nucleus that contains genetic information

- Researchers at the University of California, Irvine, are studying how eating fewer calories every day can slow the aging process. This study has shown dramatic° effects in laboratory animals. So far, scientists do not agree that eating fewer calories can slow aging in human beings.

°major

- Scientists at the National Aging Research Institute in Melbourne, Australia, are investigating how health problems affect advanced age.° Their research includes the delayed healing° of skin wounds, chronic° pain, and Alzheimer's disease.[2]

°very old people / getting better
°persistent

[2]Alzheimer's disease destroys a patient's brain cells, producing gradual loss of memory.

Researchers now ask if there is an upper° age limit beyond which   maximum
no person could survive?° No, says Dr. Kenneth Manton, a professor   live
and research director in Durham, North Carolina, in the United States.
He argues that for this to be true, there would have to be a single°   one
process where all the body's organs and cells stop functioning at one
time. Instead, many different factors determine life span. Based on current studies, Manton feels that the upper limit is 130 to 135 years even
without major medical discoveries. With genetic reengineering° or   changing genes
other medical interventions,° he feels those numbers could go higher.   discoveries

---

Facts About Life Expectancies°   expected life spans

- The average life expectancy at birth around the world is 65
  years. This number ranges from more than 75 years in devel-
  oping° countries to 52 years in the world's least developed   poorer
  nations.
- At least 120 countries now have a life expectancy at birth of
  more than 60 years. In 1980, that was true in fewer than 100
  countries.
- Japan has the world's highest life expectancy, nearly 80 years.
  The lowest, in Sierra Leone, is only 40 years.
- In Africa, at least 18 countries still have a life expectancy at
  birth of 50 years or less.
- Women can expect to live an average of four years longer than
  men. There is only a one-year difference in Southeast Asia,
  and an average of eight years in Europe.

Source: World Health Organization

LEARNING ACTIVITIES

A. Check your comprehension

Answer the items below according to information in the reading selection.

1. What was special about Ms. Jeanne Calment?
2. Name four countries where researchers are studying how to extend the human
   life span. Name one special interest of each research group.
3. According to Dr. Manton, what determines how long we will live?
4. What will be the upper age limit of human beings in the future?

5. Write the number of years people are expected to live in each of the following regions or countries. Then read them out loud.

REGION OR COUNTRY	LIFE EXPECTANCY
World	_____ years
Japan	_____ years
Africa	_____ years
Sierra Leone	_____ years
Developing countries	_____ years
Least developed countries	_____ years

B. Everything is relative

If you want to predict how long you will live, it is important to know some of your family history. Think of your four grandparents (two on your father's side of the family and two on your mother's side). Complete the paragraph below with some words from the following list.

> major, older, younger, healthier, weaker, higher, upper, lower

I am a (man / woman) and I am _____ years old. I am interested in knowing how long I will live. In my family, the _____ age limit is. . . .

On my father's side, my grandfather is now _____ years old (died at age _____). My grandmother is _____ years old (died at age _____). He/She is _____ and looks much _____ (was _____ and looked much _____).

On my mother's side, my grandfather is now _____ years old (died at age _____). My grandmother is _____ years old (died at age _____). He/She is _____ and looks much _____ (was _____ and looked much _____).

In my country, there are more _____ than _____ people and life expectancy is _____ than twenty years ago.

In conclusion, I think I will live to be about _____ years old, provided I don't smoke or have a _____ disease.

C. Amateur scientists

You may have studied some biology or genetics in school. Prepare a brief explanation of one structure or one function of a structure in the list below. If possible, use an illustration or diagram to make your presentation easier to understand.

DESCRIBE:	a cell	a cell's nucleus	a tissue	chromosomes
	genes	telomeres	DNA	genetic engineering

D. Traditional medicines

Every culture has many medicines or remedies for common problems. For each problem below, say what you or a relative normally do or do not do. Afterwards, compare your answers with those of a classmate.

EXAMPLE: stomach ache

I don't eat for 5 hours but I drink some hot tea.
My grandmother puts a warm blanket on her stomach and eats some soup.

	ME	MY RELATIVE
1. stomach ache	_____	_____
2. headache	_____	_____
3. skin burn	_____	_____
4. chest cold	_____	_____
5. head cold	_____	_____
6. food poisoning	_____	_____
7. stomach cramps	_____	_____
8. eye infection	_____	_____
9. ear infection	_____	_____
10. skin rash	_____	_____

E. How long will you live?

Take this test and find out.

1. Start with 72.   _72_
2. Male? −3   _____   Female? +4   _____
3. Live in a big city? −2   _____   Live in a small city? +4   _____
4. Work in an office? −2   _____   Do heavy physical work? +3   _____
5. Exercise regularly? +4   _____
6. Married, or live with a friend? +4   _____
7. Sleep more than ten hours daily? −4   _____
8. Nervous or aggressive? −4   _____
9. Paid a fine last year? −1   _____
10. Earn over US $50,000 a year? −1   _____
11. Have a college education? +1   _____   Have a graduate or professional degree? +2   _____
12. Over age 65 and still working? +3   _____
13. Grandfather or grandmother lived to 85? +2   _____

All four grandparents lived to 80? +6 ____

Either parent died of a stroke before 50? −4 ____

Close relative has or had cancer, heart condition, or diabetes? −3 ____

14. Smoke over two packages of cigarettes daily? −8 ____

One or two packages? −6 ____ One-half to one package? −3 ____

15. Drink about a quarter bottle of liquor daily? −1 ____

16. Man over 40 who has annual checkup (medical examination)? +2 ____

Woman who has annual gynecological checkup (medical examination for women)? +2 ____

17. Overweight by

50 pounds? −8 ____

30–40 pounds? −4 ____

10–30 pounds? −2 ____

18. Your age:

30–40: +2 ____

40–50: +3 ____

50–70: +4 ____

Over 70: +5 ____

19. Conclusion: I will live to be at least ____ years old.

F. Charting the future

1. Make a list of activities that you would do if you could live for 200 years.

2. Rank these items in the order of their importance to you, making the most important item number one.

3. Make a time chart from 0 to 200 years, showing the activities that you want to do in relationship to when you would like to do them.

EXAMPLE:

AGE	ITEM
0–22 years	Live a happy childhood
	Attend elementary and secondary school
	Study to be an engineer
30–65	Work as an engineer
	Get married
66–69	Go back to college
	Study journalism
70–100	Work as a journalist
	Travel around the world
101–?	?

4. Compare your time chart with a classmate's chart.

5. Analyze your charts. Are they similar or different? Justify your choices.

G. Small-group discussion

1. If people could live to be an average age of 175, what would the world be like? Using your imagination, complete each sentence below.

> If people could live to be 175 years old,
>   a. the population of the world would . . .
>   b. children would probably . . .
>   c. the size of many families would . . .
>   d. natural resources such as land, air, and oil would . . .
>   e. space exploration would most likely . . .
>   f. transportation such as cars, buses, and trucks would . . .
>   g. food would definitely . . .
>   h. technology certainly would . . .
>   i. the religions of the world would . . .
>   j. the economic situation in my country would . . .
>   k. the United Nations probably would . . .

2. Discuss your answers to the following questions.
    a. In your opinion, would it be better to live longer?
    b. Should a world agency decide who should live longer?
    c. Do humans have the right to change natural processes in the world?

H. Why do you suppose . . . ?

The test in activity (E) is a way to determine how long you might live. Discuss the following true statements with a classmate.

> Why do you suppose that . . .
>   1. men usually do not live as long as women?
>   2. people who live in small cities often live longer than residents of large cities?
>   3. married people tend to live longer than single people?
>   4. it is unhealthy to sleep ten hours or more every day?
>   5. people whose grandparents lived to an old age have a good chance of living a long time, too?
>   6. the more overweight people are, the younger they die.

I. Long life, at what price?

Before she died, Madame Calment was blind for a long time. Ask your classmates or friends to choose what problems in the list they would accept in exchange for living longer. Then write a summary and report your findings to your class.

EXAMPLE: To live for ten extra years, I would prefer to be (blind, deaf, unable to walk, unable to speak, unable to work, unable to eat good food, extremely thin, extremely obese, extremely sick).

Begin your report like this: For ten extra years of life, (some / most) of my friends would prefer to be . . . On the average, many classmates prefer to be . . . Fewer people prefer to be . . . Only two persons prefer to be . . . However, nobody wants to be . . .

J. My life goals

1. Imagine that you now are 200 years old and have done the activities that you ranked in your chart in activity (F). Write a composition of your memoirs, telling the most important things that happened concerning each of the items you ranked.

BEGIN LIKE THIS: I was born in _____ on _____ _____,
(place)   (month)   (number)

19_____ . . .
(year)

2. Now let's be realistic.
   a. Make a realistic life chart that outlines your life goals, and the estimated time that it will take you to achieve them.
   b. Use your chart as a basis for writing a composition about what you want to do in your lifetime and how you intend to realize your goals.

K. The oldest person I know

Describe the oldest person you know and explain what he or she does to keep well. Think of what scientists are discovering about aging now and give your opinion about what your elderly friend does correctly or incorrectly to have lived for so long.

EXAMPLE: The oldest person I know is my Uncle Muhammad. He eats lots of yogurt, drinks lots of coffee, takes a nap after lunch, and sometimes he eats lamb. I also think he eats fewer calories than younger people do.

VOCABULARY

Extending the Human Life Span

Nouns

actress	developed nations	health	materials	role
age limit	developing countries	herbs	medicines	science
aging	difference	human beings	number	scientists
aging process	discoveries	human tissue	organs	section
Alzheimer's disease	effects	institute	pain	skin wounds
average	factors	interest	politician	technology
birth	facts	interventions	possibilities	telomere
calories	fields	key question	process	trend
cells	free radicals	laboratory	reengineering	
century	genes	life expectancies	research	
chromosomes	healing	life span	researchers	

Adjectives

advanced	different	highest	national	single
Chinese	dramatic	human	oldest	special
chronic	exciting	major	organic	traditional
current	famous	maximum	shorter	upper
delayed	genetic	medical		

Verbs

affect	expect	grow	isolate	show
agree	explore	include	matter	slow
argue	extend	increase	protect	survive
continue	function	investigate	range	try
determine				

Adverbs

especially	nearly	probably	slowly	unusually

Proper Nouns

Africa	Europe	Jeanne Calment	Southeast Asia
Arles, France	Hong Kong	Melbourne, Australia	Sussex, England
Dr. Kenneth Manton	Irvine, California	Sierra Leone	United States
Durham, North Carolina	Japan		

Expressions

after all	around the world	so far	to catch the public's attention	to pay attention

Vocabulary Review
Unit V

A. Word sets

In each word set below, cross out the word that does *not* belong to it. Then explain why you crossed out the word in each set.

EXAMPLE: ~~aging~~ / sperm / egg / union

The noun *aging* does not refer to reproduction.

1. uterus / woman / female / sperm   _____
2. Asia / Africa / Hong Kong / Australia   _____
3. process / cloning / replica / duplication   _____
4. genes / chromosomes / cells / calories   _____
5. leader / soldier / politician / scientist   _____
6. Sierra Leone / North Carolina / England / France   _____
7. to grow / to reproduce / to increase / to isolate   _____
8. to research / to investigate / to fertilize / to explore   _____

B. Reading for meaning

Read the selection below. Then complete the reading with appropriate words and phrases from the following list.

probably, difference, Therefore, healthy, centuries, technology, reproduction, In short, human, argue, exciting, dramatic, Immortality, affect, major, methods, All around the world, health, human beings, protect, numbers, medical doctors, chronic, especially, grow, expect, leaders, nearly, survive

Immortality

"Immortality" means to live forever. How would you like to be so _____ that you would never die? You would live for thousands of _____. Isn't that idea _____ yet scary? _____ would certainly _____ our world in many ways. How? Here are several examples.

Human life. Billions and billions of _____ would live on our planet. There would _____ be few villages or towns; instead, there would be great _____ of large urban areas. Many farms would be necessary to _____ enough food to feed all the people. If _____ were in short supply, _____ care would become a _____ problem;

_____ diseases could be a destructive factor. One might _____ that advanced _____ would offer some assistance particularly in slowing the population growth. Political _____ would try many _____ to control human _____ but their efforts might prove to be _____ impossible and certainly unpopular.

Competition. _____ people would compete for nearly everything, _____ for food, housing, and jobs. _____ , people would be so busy trying to _____ that there would be little time to form friendships. _____ , people would _____ more with each other and they would not trust one another.

Destruction. If people were immortal, there would be no world peace. The United Nations would use _____ means to _____ people from destroying each other through war. But its efforts might not make a _____ for it could be too late. Imagine how _____ immortality could change our global village!

C. Which do you prefer?

Mark or write in the blank *one* preference to complete each sentence below. Then read aloud your preferences to a classmate. Your teacher may ask you to explain why you chose certain preferences.

1. I like . . .
   ____ healthy foods   ____ high technology   _____
2. I prefer to eat foods that are grown . . .
   ____ organically   ____ artificially   _____
3. I like to grow . . .
   ____ my own herbs   ____ medicinal plants   _____
4. I am in favor of cloning animals . . .
   ____ for food   ____ for pets   _____
5. Soon it may be possible to . . .
   ____ clone humans   ____ live on other planets   _____
6. I'd like a clone of . . .
   ____ myself   ____ my best friend   _____
7. Reproduction should be . . .
   ____ always natural   ____ sometimes artificial   _____
8. Genetic engineering is . . .
   ____ dangerous   ____ exciting   _____
9. I think that male and female roles are . . .
   ____ changing quickly   ____ changing slowly   _____
10. I can't imagine a world without . . .
   ____ any age limit   ____ technology   _____

D. Getting to know you

Ask a classmate the questions below. Write down his or her answers. When you finish, your classmate should ask *you* the questions.

1. Who or what really matters to you in life? What have been some very exciting events in your life?
2. What effect does medical technology have in your life?
3. What can be done to protect scientists from destroying our global village? How can you participate in that process?
4. What can our political leaders do to bring peace to our world society?
5. I will say some adjectives. Tell me if the adjectives describe you. Say "Yes," "No," or "It depends" (and explain on what it depends).

    single   famous   political   traditional
    healthy   special

E. Human life sciences

Complete the crossword puzzle on the next page.

Human life sciences

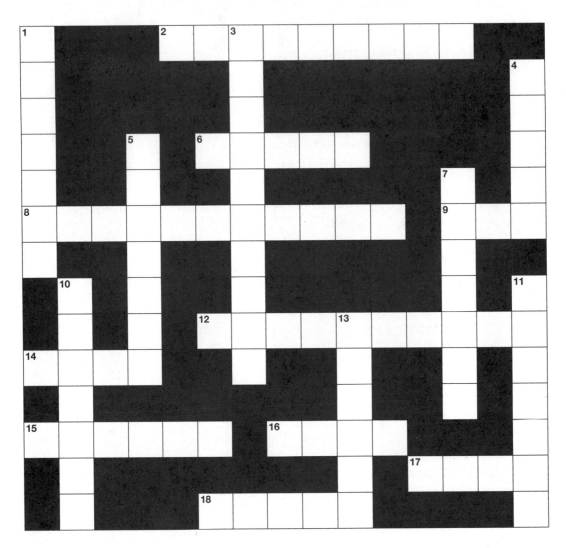

ACROSS

2. A large city in southern Australia
6. A person who gives something to charity
8. Living forever
9. The female cell
12. The opposite of natural
14. The opposite of female
15. The female organ where babies grow
16. To become larger
17. Hurt or discomfort
18. Plants used as spices

DOWN

1. Persistent
3. Where test–tube babies are made
4. Getting older
5. To separate
7. Getting better in health
10. In good health
11. Making an exact duplicate of a plant, animal, or human being
13. Well-known

UNIT VI

BUSINESS AFFAIRS

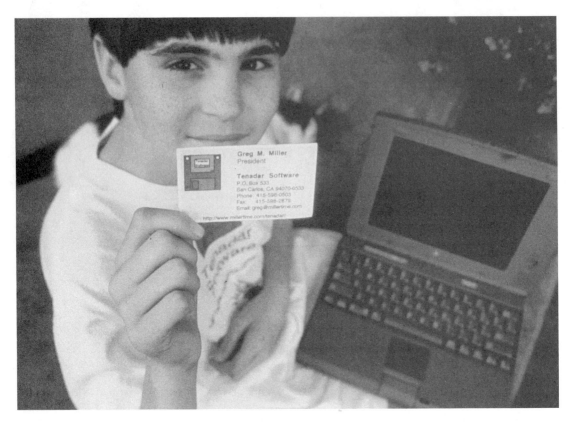

Gregory Miller, 13, started a company called Tenador Software after inventing a computer game.

11 Mini Computer Moguls[1]

Impressed by the cogent° technical advice Minneapolis resident   persuasive
Trent Eisenberg passed on° to some members of an online help forum,°   gave / group
computer powerhouse Compaq approached him about a job at the
company's headquarters in Houston. But Compaq was forced to with-
draw the offer when a crucial° detail about Eisenberg came to light°:   important / was discovered
He was just 14. Two years later, Eisenberg now runs his own technical
support° company, F1 Computer, (named for the help key on DOS-   consulting
based computer keyboards). "I might be interested in getting a corporate job in a few years, after college," he says. "But this is just right for
me now."

    Eisenberg is among an increasing number of 10-something°   about 10 or 11 years old
kids who are running their own computer-related businesses—and,
for the most part, thriving° at it. "Many kids in suburban homes   are successful
have grown up operating very powerful computers, so technology
is second nature° to them in a way that it's not to many adults," says   natural
Gene DeRose, president of Jupiter Communications, a high-tech research firm based in New York. "They're just doing what kids did
10, 15 years ago to make money—using the tools available to them."
[. . .]

    Danny Kalmick, the 14-year-old president of Kalmick & Co.
Computing in Seal Beach, Calif., took his first step toward becoming a neighborhood computer guru° at age 11, when he disassem-   expert
bled his first PC (a 486/DX2) to inspect its motherboard. When neigh-
bors called him for computer advice a year later, Kalmick saw a
business opportunity. "I realized I was offering the same kind of services that older guys with degrees were getting $150 an hour for,"
says Kalmick. "I felt like, as a kid, I could do the job more cheaply."
So he printed up business cards, secured a license, and took out an
ad in a neighborhood directory°: he now has about 10 regular clients,   telephone book

works six to 10 hours a week, and earns $20 an hour custom-
building computer systems and trouble-shooting° tech problems. [. . .]   solving

    Cut rates° are certainly an asset in the marketplace, but so, argue   Low prices
many young entrepreneurs,° is age: Kids aren't as intimidating° to   business people /
work with, they say, as their more senior counterparts. "We're profes-   frightening
sional, of course, but we are just kids, and people feel like they can talk
with us and ask us whatever they want without being embarrassed,"
says Charles Ross, 18, vice president of Pixelstorm Inc., a Web services
company that develops marketing sites for local businesses. Ross runs
the firm with his twin brother, James, and their friend Matthew Baylis,
17, out of the Ross family home in Orlando, Fla. "Plus,° a lot of our   In addition
clients tell us that they would rather work with us because we've grown
up with the technology and have a solid handle on it.°" [. . .]   understand it well

LEARNING ACTIVITIES

A. Check your comprehension

1. Complete the following chart, showing the name of each young business entrepreneur, his current age in the reading, the name of his company, and where his business
   is located.

NAME	AGE	NAME OF COMPANY	LOCATION OF BUSINESS
Trent Eisenberg	_____	F1 Computer	_____, Minnesota
_____	14	_____	Seal Beach, _____
Charles Ross	_____	Pixelstorm Inc.	_____, Florida
Matthew Baylis	_____	_____	_____

2. Complete the following statements according to the reading selection.

   a. The title of the reading, "Mini Computer Moguls," refers to . . .
      - young computer entrepreneurs.
      - new kinds of computer companies.
      - expensive, high-tech inventions.
      - very small high-speed computers.

b. Trent Eisenberg could not work for the Compaq computer company because . . .
- Compaq didn't want to hire him.
- he wanted a very high salary.
- he was too young for the job.
- he didn't have enough experience.

c. Most children who run their own computer business are . . .
- very rich.
- successful.
- unsuccessful.
- inexperienced.

d. All of the "mini computer moguls" in the reading . . .
- are very good friends.
- work for other people.
- work in the United States.
- do business with each other.

B. Increasing your word power

Write at least two words or expressions associated with those listed below.

EXAMPLE: business = firm, technical support, opportunity

1. keyboard	**9.** entrepreneur
2. Web site	**10.** online forum
3. advice	**11.** 10 hours a week
4. mogul	**12.** to make money
5. 10-something	**13.** second nature
6. directory	**14.** a solid handle
7. powerhouse	**15.** high-tech
8. modem	

C. Computer jargon

1. Study the meaning of the computer-related words on the next page.

2. Your teacher will help you pronounce these words correctly.

3. Label the parts of the computer system with their appropriate names from the list.

computer	diskette	on/off switch	on/off switch	mousepad
motherboard	on/off switch	sound system	keyboard	printer
CD-ROM drive	monitor	speakers	help key	paper tray
CD-ROM disk	monitor stand	speaker cords	number keyboard	on/off switch
hard drive	screen	amplifier	mouse	

D. Twelve little dwarfs

Snow White had seven Dwarfs to help her. The mini computer moguls have twelve function keys to help them. If you have a computer, draw its keyboard, and explain what each one of the function keys do for you.

EXAMPLE: If you press the F1 key, you get help with your program.

E. Entering the workforce

To describe what people are doing at present, use a form of **to be** (*am, is, are*) + **-ing.** Complete the sentences below using verbs from the list provided. Note that sometimes adverbs like *also, already,* and *always* are inserted between the forms of **to be** and the **-ing** verb forms.

EXAMPLE: I **am** *already* **preparing** for a corporate job after college.

to use	to offer	to run	to custom-build
to thrive	to plan	to fix	to trouble-shoot
to become			to operate

1. Trent Eisenberg _____ _____ to get a corporate job when he is older. I _____ also _____ to get a technical/corporate/professional job later.

2. Trent Eisenberg is only a kid but he _____ _____ his own computer business and _____ _____ at it.

3. Most mini computer moguls grew up with computers so they _____ always _____ or _____ very expensive equipment.

4. Trent, Charles, and Danny _____ _____ what kids did ten or fifteen years ago to make money: They _____ _____ the tools available to them.

5. All over the country, children like Danny Kalmick, eleven, _____ _____ neighborhood gurus. They _____ _____ the same kinds of service computer technicians offer.

6. My cousins Annette and Chris _____ now _____ a complete network for the neighborhood library. They _____ also _____ for a local law firm.

F. Two mini computer moguls and me

Compare yourself with Trent Eisenberg and Danny Kalmick, two young entrepreneurs mentioned in the reading. Read the statements about these boys, then complete the personalized sentences about yourself. You can use these sentences to write to an employer.

1. Trent Eisenberg is a resident of Minneapolis, Minnesota.

   My name is _____. I'm a resident of _____.

2. Trent is interested in getting a corporate job in a few years.

   I'm interested in getting a _____ job in _____.

3. Technology is second nature to young Trent.

   _____ is second nature to me.

4. Right now Trent runs his own business.

   Right now I'm working for _____. (I'm not working.)

5. Danny Kalmick works six to 10 hours a week.

   I usually work _____ hours per week. (I don't work.)

6. Danny is fourteen years old and earns US $20 an hour at his job.

I am _____ years old and earn US $_____ an hour at my job. (I don't get paid for my work.)

7. Danny's job is custom-building computer systems and trouble-shooting technical problems.

My job is _____ and _____ .

G. Computer power

1. If you have a computer, explain to a group of classmates what programs you have.

EXAMPLE: I have Microsoft *Word* for word processing and I have _____ for navigating the Internet. I also draw with _____ , and listen to music with _____ . When I am bored, I play _____ on my computer.

2. A computer is an excellent workhorse. With two classmates, make a list of tasks that you know can be done on a computer. Then make another list of additional tasks that you would like computers to do for you.

EXAMPLES: Can be done: keeping records, . . .

I would like done: resolving all math problems, . . .

3. From the list below, choose the kinds of classes you would take to use a computer more efficiently. You may also add your own selection. Share your choices with your classmates and indicate why you need the classes.

EXAMPLE: I would take a class on tax computation because my father needs help with tax preparation.

word processing	plan drafting for architects	hospital administration
Web page creation	spreadsheets like Lotus® 1,2,3	school administration
Web site searching	travel and hotel reservations	warehouse/stock control
payroll/salaries programs	flight reservations	?
design programs for engineers	restaurant stock and menus	

H. My own company

Imagine that you are going to form a business like the mini computer moguls. Answer the questions on the next page.

Your Company

1. What services would your company offer?
2. What name would you choose for your company?
3. Where would it be located?
4. What would your position be in the company?
5. What would your business card look like? (Make a simple drawing.)

Your Employees

1. Would you have one or more partners in your company? If so, who would they be?
2. About how many employees would you hire for your company?
3. About how many employees would be male? How many female? How old would they be?
4. What kind of expertise would they have?
5. What would be a typical employee's weekly salary?
6. What fringe benefits would you provide them (e.g., health insurance, paid vacation)?

Your Clients

1. Who would most of your clients be? Their ages?
2. How would you attract them to your business?
3. Why would your clients come to your company?

I. Pro and con

Most situations have pros and cons—that is, advantages and disadvantages. Answer the following questions in writing, then compare your written answers with those of a classmate.

Business People

1. What advantages do very young entrepreneurs have over adult business people?
2. What disadvantages do the mini computer moguls have compared with their older colleagues?

Their Clients

1. What advantages do the clients of each age group have?
2. What disadvantages do these customers have?
3. If you needed computer advice, would you prefer to ask it of a neighborhood child guru or an adult in a technical support company? Why?

VOCABULARY

Mini Computer Moguls

Nouns

ad	computer moguls	guys	members	research firm
adults	computer systems	headquarters	motherboard	resident
advice	computers	help forum	neighborhood	services
asset	corporate job	help key	neighborhood directory	step
business cards	counterparts	homes	neighbors	support
business opportunity	cut rates	hour	number	tech problems
businesses	degrees	job	offer	technology
clients	detail	kids	PC	tools
company	entrepreneurs	kind	people	twin brother
computer advice	family home	license	powerhouse	vice president
computer guru	firm	marketing sites	president	years
computer keyboards	friend	marketplace		

Adjectives

available	embarrassed	increasing	powerful	suburban
cogent	first	intimidating	professional	technical
computer-related	14-year-old	local	regular	10-something
crucial	high-tech	older	senior	young
DOS-based				

Verbs

approach	call	impress	run	tell
argue	custom-build	inspect	say	thrive at
ask	develop	make	secure	trouble-shoot
be based	disassemble	offer	see	use
be forced	earn	operate	take	want
be interested in	feel like	pass on	take out	withdraw
be named for	get	print up	talk	work
become	grow up	realize		

Adverbs

certainly	cheap	later

Proper Nouns

Charles Ross	Houston	Matthew Baylis	Pixelstorm Inc.
Compaq	James	Minneapolis	Seal Beach, Calif.
Danny Kalmick	Jupiter Communications	New York	Trent Eisenberg
F1 Computer	Kalmick & Co. Computing	Orlando, Fla.	Web services company
Gene DeRose			

Expressions

after college	of course	second nature	to come to light	to have a solid handle
for the most part	online	to be just right		

Petrona Towers.

12 Tower Power

$\mathbf{F}$or a century, the United States was the world leader of the tallest buildings: skyscrapers. But in 1996, the Petronas Towers of Kuala Lumpur, Malaysia, challenged this leadership. The Petronas are 1,483-foot tall (452 meters), 33 feet (10 meters) taller than the Sears Tower in Chicago, which was until then the tallest of them all. However, the gracefully tapered° US$1.2 billion Petronas will not wear the high-rise crown for a long time. In 1998, construction started on the 1,509-foot-tall (459.5 meters) Shanghai World Financial Center, which will be 26 feet (7.5 meters) taller than the Petronas Towers. Amazing! °shaped

These "temples of commerce" are the physical manifestation of the current preoccupation° with business. At the beginning of the U.S. Civil War, tall office buildings transformed° residential Wall Street in Manhattan into the business district and the financial power house it still is. Then, at the end of the 19th century, the invention of the elevator made eight and 10-story buildings practical. But it was not until the introduction of steel-beam construction that real skyscrapers became possible in 1885. Of course, high-speed elevators, mass-produced steel, the telephone, and electric lights all contributed to reaching higher and higher as land became more and more expensive in crowded 20th-century cities. °interest °changed

Skyscrapers thus are the world's most universal architectural symbol for rich industrialists° and expanding corporations. The skyscraper is an easy way of having the whole operation under one roof. It was also the perfect advertisement of major companies' success: The Singer Building went up in 1908, the Metropolitan Life in 1909, the Woolworth in 1913. In the 30s° more were to come and skyscrapers topped 1,000 feet (304.8 meters): The beautiful Chrysler Building opened in 1930 and when the Empire State Building was finished in 1931, the world stood in awe of° such a magnificent symbol of New York for almost 40 years. Then the twin towers of the World Trade Center shot up° on the banks of the Hudson River in the early 70s. °business people °Between 1930 and 1939 °was surprised by °were built

At present, the Petronas command° similar admiration. Designed   demand
by César Pelli, the renowned Argentinean architect based in New York,
the Petronas Towers gleam° by day and glitter° by night. They share   shine / sparkle
the Islamic influence and geometric patterns of the surrounding high-
rises. But they also radiate a sleek,° masculine aura and project a colos-   polished
sal,° powerful prestige. Unrivaled° giants, they can be seen from as far   very big / Unique
as 12.5 miles (20 kilometers) away.

At the end of the 20th century, almost every cityscape—not only
Kuala Lumpur's—has been changed by high-rises around the world.
The Jin Mao celebrates Shanghai, the Commerzbank building marks
Frankfurt and the 95-story Millennium Tower may leave its mark in
London, too. But none will be such a personal symbol as an astound-
ing Hong Kong tower still on the drawing board.° Proposed by Nina   in the planning stages
Wang, the richest woman in Asia, the skyscraper will cost a cool US$1
billion. Nina, who has a personal fortune estimated at US$3.3 billion,
likes miniskirts and BIG business. She plans the tallest building in Hong
Kong as a monument to the city's future. The building's name? Nina
Tower, of course. She told London's *The Times:* "I will look up and say:
'That's my building.'"

In fact, if everything goes as planned, by 2000, nine of the world's
tallest buildings will be located in Asia. But all over our global village,
these "cities within cities" will stand as monuments to the 20th century's exhilarating° race for the sky.   exciting

LEARNING ACTIVITIES

A. Check your comprehension

Match the events in the right-hand column according to their time line in the left-hand
column. Base your decisions on the reading.

TIME LINE		EVENT
1. ____	U.S. Civil War era	**a.** Asia will have nine of world's tallest buildings
2. ____	End of 19th century	**b.** Elevator invented, 10-story buildings built
3. ____	1885 to present	**c.** Empire State is world's tallest building
4. ____	Early 20th century	**d.** Most large cities have tall skyscrapers
5. ____	Beginning of 1930s	**e.** Skyscrapers built over 1,000-feet tall
6. ____	1931 to late 1960s	**f.** Steel-beam construction is used in skyscrapers
7. ____	Early 1970s	**g.** Tall office buildings built in Manhattan
8. ____	End of 20th century	**h.** Telephones and electric lights in high-rises
9. ____	Beginning of 2000s	**i.** World Trade Center built on Hudson River

Fill in the missing information in the chart below according to the reading.

	SKYSCRAPER	YEAR BUILT	CITY	HEIGHT
1.	Nina Tower	2000	_____	unknown
2.	World Financial Center	1998	Shanghai	_____ feet
3.	_____	1996	Kuala Lumpur	1,483 feet
4.	Sears Tower	_____	Chicago	1,454 feet
5.	World Trade Center	1973	_____	1,360 feet
6.	Empire State Building	1931	_____	1,250 feet
7.	_____	1930	New York	1,046 feet
8.	Woolworth Building	_____	New York	792 feet
9.	Metropolitan Life Building	_____	New York	720 feet
10.	_____	1908	New York	410 feet

Answer the following questions.

1. Why is "Tower Power" an appropriate title for this reading?
2. Which skyscraper mentioned in the reading would you most like to visit? Why?
3. Who is the richest woman in Asia? Where does she live? What does she want to do with her money?

B. Talking numbers

To become a fluent speaker of English, you must say numbers clearly.[1]

EXAMPLE: The Nina Tower will cost US$1 billion.
["The Nina Tower will cost one billion U.S. dollars."]

In English, numerical expressions go before the nouns they describe. Years are broken into two parts and are given as tens, except years between 2000 and 2009.

EXAMPLE: 1989 (written form)
nineteen eighty-nine (oral form)

Note that prices and dimensions given in stories or feet change depending on whether the expression is an adjective (singular form) or a noun (plural form).

---

[1]If you speak another European language or follow European usage, one billion in American English may be 1,000 million in your culture.

EXAMPLE: ADJECTIVES
a *5-story* house
a *45-foot* house
the gracefully tapered *US$1.2 billion* Petronas Tower
NOUNS
The house is *five stories* tall.
The house is *45 feet* tall.
The gracefully tapered Petronas cost *US$1.2 billion.*

With the help of your teacher, read aloud the following sentences, paying attention to the pronunciation of dates and figures.

1. At the end of the 19th century, the invention of the elevator made eight and 10-story buildings practical.
2. By the year 2015, land in cities will be very expensive.
3. The Singer Building went up in 1908, the Metropolitan Life in 1909, the Woolworth in 1913.
4. In the 30s, skyscrapers topped 1,000 feet or 304.8 meters.
5. The two Petronas Towers cost US$1.2 billion.
6. In 1998, construction started on the 1,509-foot-tall (or 459.5-meter-tall) Shanghai World Financial Center.
7. The Shanghai World Financial Center is 26 feet or 7.5 meters taller than the Petronas Towers.
8. The Shanghai World Financial Center is 1,509 feet or 459.5 meters tall.
9. The sleek 1-billion dollar Nina Tower will be built in the 21st century.
10. The two giant Petronas Towers can be seen from 12.5 miles (20 kilometers) away.

C. Increasing your word power

Two nouns. In English, you can use nouns to build "meaning towers." Two (or more) nouns together can describe someone or something accurately. In some cases, two nouns may become a single word.

EXAMPLE: power house ⟶ powerhouse

1. Fill in the missing part in the nouns below. Look at the reading selection in this chapter to help you.

2. Afterwards, write sentences using the nouns that you formed.

EXAMPLE: city district with much business activity: *business* district
Also: businessman, business acumen, business deal, business course

a. _____ board   f. sky_____

b. office _____   g. high-rise _____

c. _____ leader   h. Nina _____

d. _____ house   i. _____ district

e. _____beam   j. Empire _____ _____

Hyphenated adjectives. You can also use hyphenated adjectives to describe people and things.

1. Fill in the missing part in the adjectives below. Look at the reading selection in this chapter to help you.

   EXAMPLE: an inexpensive project = a *low-cost* project

   1. A very expensive apartment: a _____-_____ apartment

   2. A building that rises very high: a _____-_____ building

   3. A motor that runs at high speeds: a _____-_____ engine

   4. Steel produced in massive amounts: _____-_____ steel

   5. Very strong beams made of steel: _____-_____ construction

Word families. You can guess the meaning of new words by trying to place it in a "word family."

1. Complete the following word family chart.

NOUN	VERB	PERSON	ADJECTIVE
1. architecture	xxxxxxxxxx	_____	architectural
2. finances	_____	financier	_____
3. _____	xxxxxxxxxx	xxxxx	global
4. person	_____	xxxxx	_____
5. residence	to reside	resident	_____
6. plan	_____	planner	planned (community)
7. admiration	to admire	_____	admirable
8. _____	to construct	_____	constructive
9. _____	to incorporate	xxxxxxxx	corporate

2. Complete the following paragraph with appropriate words from the chart above.

Several _____ features define the skyline in Kuala Lumpur, a city with a strong Islamic influence. Of course, the _____ Petronas Towers dominate the downtown section. This _____ project required unique _____ solutions and strong _____ construction. At night the Towers shine brightly, as if smiling with pride in the sky. _____ from many countries come to take pictures of the Towers to remember them. Unfortunately, only _____ executives and special guests can enter because no visits are _____ for the public.

D. Build me a skyscraper!

Imagine that you are an architect who has been hired to design a skyscraper. First, make some notes on the twelve items below regarding your skyscraper. Then discuss your plans with those of a classmate.

1. **Name:** What will be the name of your skyscraper? Example: Nina Tower
2. **Location:** country, city, specific building site
3. **Height:** in feet or meters and number of stories
4. **Design:** What will your skyscraper look like when it is finished?
5. **Materials:** What materials will you use in its construction?
6. **Project cost:** What will your skyscraper cost in U.S. dollars and/or in your country's currency?
7. **Funding source:** Who will supply the money to build your skyscraper?
8. **Functions:** What will your building be used for—offices, apartments, shops, medical center, etc.?
9. **Features:** Will your building have high-speed elevators, TV security monitors, etc.?
10. **Opening year:** Estimate the number of years you will need to build it.
11. **Opening activities:** What activities do you plan for opening day?
12. **Invited guests:** Who will be your guests on that day?

E. Cityscapes

Today, as in ancient times, certain cities are financial powerhouses. With two classmates, write a report of a financial center you know or would like to work in. Try to use the following expressions from the reading:

business district	the . . . Building shot up on . . .
financial power house	. . . wears the high-rise crown
temple(s) of commerce	the perfect advertisement of success
more and more expensive	if everything goes as planned, by 2005 . . .
people stood in awe of . . .	

Include the following in your report:

1. The period (for example, the eighties, the 1990s) when the city and its main businesses were established.

2. Describe the main buildings or construction projects that have marked or celebrated the rise of the city. Include the names of architectural firms, dimensions, materials, shapes, colors, and effects on those watching (for example: it glitters, it shines, it races for the sky, it erases everything else from the horizon, it radiates an aura of . . .).

3. Describe which corporations or corporate groups are based in this city. Explain which families or groups of people have the most assets. If possible, mention how they earned their fortunes.

F. Make way for the future!

In the twenty-first century, regions other than Europe and North America will be highly developed. With several classmates, make some plans for these new financial powers in our global village. Explain why you are making this prediction.

Useful Terms and Expressions			
architects	educated work force	technical know-how	global interdependence
engineers	huge banks	population growth	multinational companies
designers	skyscrapers	global economy	influential financial centers
programmers	stock market	industrial output	telecommunications network
financiers	expanding business		

BEGIN LIKE THIS:

In the 21st century, (Africa / Asia) will rise as a global financial power. The conditions are already present because (Africa / Asia) has already begun . . . and supported . . . Huge banks and financial powerhouses are located in . . .

G. My dream home

1. Draw a simple plan of your dream house or apartment. Then write a description of the rooms, furniture, and decor that you want to put in it.

EXAMPLES: I want a house with three bedrooms, a kitchen, a large living room and . . .
In my bedroom I want a queen-size waterbed and . . .
In the kitchen I want yellow walls, a white tile floor and . . .

2. Discuss your dream house with a classmate. Tell him or her . . .

    a. where you want your house built, and why.

    b. what electrical appliances you want to have.

    c. with whom you want to share your house, and why.

    d. what your dream house will cost in U.S. dollars.

H. Name that skyscraper!

1. Working with a classmate, list the characteristics of a tall building in your city. Try to use some vocabulary that you learned in this chapter such as noun-noun combinations (power house), simple adjectives (geometric), hyphenated adjectives (high-cost), and verbs of visual perception (to shine).

2. Now form a group with several other classmates. By listening to your description of the tall building you have chosen, your classmates will try to guess the name of the building and its location.

I. Temples of commerce

Not all temples of commerce reside in skyscrapers. Some are markets, city blocks, or even electronic Web sites. Write a description or a comparison between human-size or electronic and superhuman-size temples of commerce.

Useful Terms and Expressions	
as e-mail gets more and more common . . .	as information gets more and more accessible . . .
as land gets more and more scarce and expensive . . .	because . . . is a local, not a global business . . .

J. Power houses in miniskirts

The richest woman in Asia, Nina Wang, will soon build her own skyscraper. Are there wealthy female executives in your country, too? Do some research about one of them. Then write a description of how she became wealthy, what her approximate net worth is, and the buildings or projects she owns and plans to build in the future. Use some expressions that you learned in this chapter.

K. Back to the drawing board

Towers may be colossal monuments to modern wealth, but often they fail as residential dwellings. With a group of three students, draw and plan a multifamily community or building that uses land wisely and provides for interaction among humans and nature. Present your ideas to the class or record your presentation as a promotional video to show to the class.

L. Reach for the sky!

This is your opportunity to describe your business ideas for the future. Get together with one or two partners and write several paragraphs to promote your business idea on the Internet. Be creative and original.

VOCABULARY

Tower Power

Nouns

admiration	commerce	influence	operation	telephone
advertisement	construction	introduction	patterns	temples
architect	corporations	invention	power	time
aura	crown	kilometers	powerhouse	tower
banks	drawing board	land	preoccupation	twin
beginning	elevator	leadership	prestige	village
building	end	lights	race	war
business	fortune	manifestation	sky	way
business district	future	miniskirts	skyscrapers	woman
century	giants	monument	steel	world
city	high-rises	name	success	world leader
cityscape	industrialists	office buildings	symbol	years

Adjectives

amazing	current	high-speed	physical	sleek
architectural	designed	higher	possible	steel-beam
Argentinean	easy	Islamic	powerful	surrounding
astounding	electric	long	practical	tall
based	exhilarating	magnificent	real	taller
beautiful	expanding	major	renowned	tallest
big	expensive	masculine	residential	tapered
civil	financial	mass-produced	rich	universal
colossal	geometric	perfect	richest	unrivaled
cool	global	personal	similar	whole
crowded	high-rise			

Verbs

become	finish	mark	reach	start
challenge	gleam	open	say	tell
command	glitter	plan	share	top
contribute	like	project	shoot up	transform
cost	look up	radiate	stand	wear
estimate	make			

Adverbs

almost   gracefully   still

Proper Nouns

Asia	Hudson River	Millennium Tower	Singer Building
César Pelli	Jin Mao	New York	*The Times*
Chicago	Kuala Lumpur	Nina Tower	United States
Chrysler Building	London	Nina Wang	Wall Street
Commerzbank	Malaysia	Petronas Towers	Woolworth
Empire State Building	Manhattan	Sears Tower	World Financial Center
Frankfurt	Metropolitan Life	Shanghai	World Trade Center
Hong Kong			

Expressions

at present	by night	more and more	of course	to stand in awe of
by day	in fact	more to come	to leave its mark	under one roof

Abbreviations

19th century   20th century   US$ 30s   70s

Vocabulary Review
Unit VI

A. Word sets

In each word set below, cross out the word that does *not* belong to it. Then explain why you crossed out the word in each set.

EXAMPLE: ~~London~~ / Minneapolis / Houston / Orlando
London is not a large American city.

1. cut rates / power / cheaply / fortune   _____
2. neighbor / elevator / telephone / computer   _____
3. residential / neighborhood / village / detail   _____
4. Kuala Lumpur / Hong Kong / Shanghai / Chicago   _____
5. business / entrepreneur / company / corporation   _____
6. temple / office building / license / skyscraper   _____
7. to glitter / to reach / to radiate / to gleam   _____
8. universal / astounding / amazing / magnificent   _____
9. corporations / companies / patterns / marketplaces   _____

B. Reading for meaning

Read the selection below. Then complete the reading with appropriate words and phrases from the following list.

business district, skyscraper, architect, earn, corporate job, residential, homes, crucial, at present, powerful, work, professional, clients, challenges, headquarters, marketplace, president, personal company, advice, high-speed

The World of Work

_____ is an important part of our lives. It gives us the food we eat, it pays our bills, and it gives direction to our lives. Let's listen to three hard-working _____ business people who are successful in their work.

"Hello! My name is Jennifer. I used to have a _____ at the _____ of an international firm in Houston, Texas, but I found that job too intimidating. Now I live in a small town in southern Vermont where I am _____ of my own _____, Computer Dynamics. With my staff of three employees, we offer computer _____ to small businesses here in New England."

"Welcome to the _____ of Hong Kong. My name is Wang Chi-ying. I work as a stockbroker in a 60-story _____ in this _____ city. Every day during the week I trade millions of dollars of stock in the world _____. All my work is performed by _____ communications because time is _____; some of my _____ make and lose millions in less than one minute."

"Nice to meet you. My name is David Liebson. I'm an _____ here in Tel Aviv. I design low-cost _____ for Jewish refugees who come to live and work in Israel. _____ I am developing a small _____ community for young families who don't _____ much money. My work _____ me a great deal but it also gives me a great deal of _____ satisfaction."

C. Which do you prefer?

Mark or write in the blank *one* preference to complete each sentence below. Then read aloud your preferences to a classmate.

1. I like visiting . . .
_____ local coffeehouses   _____ sleek high-rises   _____

2. But I don't like visiting . . .
_____ crowded cities   _____ suburban   _____
                                        neighborhoods

3. My favorite cityscape is in . . .
_____ Manhattan   _____ Hong Kong   _____

4. For me financial success is . . .
_____ very important   _____ not very important   _____

5. I'd like to work for . . .
_____ a large corporation   _____ a small business   _____

6. I'd like to own . . .
_____ a research firm   _____ a computer system   _____

7. Someday I'd like to be . . .
_____ an entrepreneur   _____ a corporate president   _____

8. There are many good business opportunities in . . .
_____ my profession   _____ my country   _____

9. High technology . . .
_____ frightens me   _____ is fascinating   _____

10. I am very interested in . . .
_____ high-tech   _____ super computers   _____
communications

D. Getting to know you

Ask a classmate the questions below. Write down his or her answers. When you finish, your classmate should ask *you* the questions. Your teacher may ask you to explain why you chose certain preferences.

1. Do you have the basic knowledge to operate a computer? If so, do you own your own computer? If so, what kind is it? If you don't have a computer, do you plan on buying one in the near future?

2. Would you consider yourself to be an entrepreneurial type of person? If so, would you like to have your own business? If so, what kind of business?

3. Do you have your own business cards? If so, please show me one. If you don't have your own business cards, do you plan on having some printed in the near future?

4. Some people think that women should not be corporate presidents. Do you agree or disagree with this idea? Why do you agree (disagree)? Do you know a successful woman who holds a high position in a corporation? If so, please tell me about her.

5. I will say some adjectives. Tell me if the adjectives describe you. Say "Yes," "No," or "It depends" (and explain on what it depends).

tall	practical	20-something	professional
young	renowned	intimidating	exhilarating
powerful			

E. Business affairs

Complete the crossword puzzle on the next page.

Business affairs

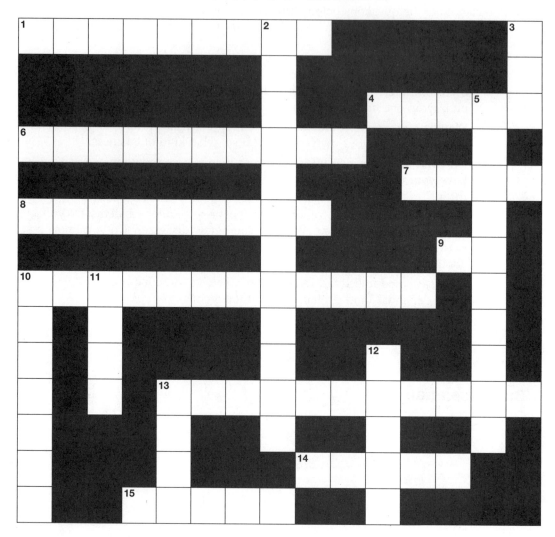

ACROSS

1. Unique, one of a kind
4. The opposite of last
6. Amazing
7. Another word for boys or men
8. Referring to money
9. The abbreviation for "personal computer"
10. Frightening, scary
13. Changed
14. The opposite of old
15. Polished

DOWN

2. Exciting
3. To obtain
5. A very tall building, especially in a city
10. To investigate
11. To speak
12. A group or gathering of professionals
13. The opposite of short

UNIT VII

THE FUTURE

13 Greenhouse Common Sense

If you are tired of inconclusive theories about global warming, join the club.° Everyone has heard that artificial greenhouse gases might cause the Earth to warm. But in the endless pro and con° on the subject . . . , neither the alarmists nor the naysayers° can prove their positions. At best,° the science of global warming is ambiguous;° at worst,° it's a realm of° computer-simulated jabber°. . . Earth's climate is simply too vast and complex for anyone yet to understand it.

    Yet while greenhouse forecasts are uncertain and likely to remain so, it is incontestable° that the chemistry of the atmosphere is changing. Airborne carbon dioxide has increased by one third since the industrial revolution and appears on its way to doubling. Altering° the atmosphere must eventually have some effect—and we may not like it, especially since even relatively mild climate change might affect the high-yield agriculture on which human prosperity° depends.

    Recognizing this, many economists—a group not normally accused of green zeal°—have begun to argue for reform. Recently more than 2,500 economists, including eight Nobel Prize winners, endorsed° a statement sponsored by the organization Redefining Progress saying that "sound economic analysis" shows greenhouse emissions° can be cut "without harming American living standards."

    . . . The history of pollution control shows that benefits usually exceed the costs. In 1972, only about one third of American lakes and rivers were safe for fishing and swimming; today, almost two thirds are safe, a stunning° improvement that occurred even during sustained economic growth. Since 1970, smog in the U.S. has diminished by nearly a third; the number of cars has almost doubled.

    . . . Of course, not every reform works well in economic terms, the Endangered Species Act being a prominent° counterexample. But

you are not alone

discussion / people who disagree

In the best of cases

not clear / in the worst of cases / it's all / nonsense talk

certain

Changing

wealth

concern for the environment

approved

gases

surprising

important

more often than not, in environmental initiatives a cycle of negative to positive occurs. First, all sides condemn° the new idea: Environmental advocates say it isn't enough; some business executives say it will be impossibly expensive. Next comes a phase of general unhappiness in which lawyers rule.° Then innovations occur—such as the invention of the catalytic converter—which made automotive smog-control practical—and efficiencies result. Ten years later both pollution and costs are declining, though this never prevents the same institutional parties from making the same gloomy° predictions about the next round of reforms.

    . . . Because artificial greenhouse gases are released mainly when fossil fuels are burned, any effort to check them will for all intents and purposes° be an energy-conservation initiative.

    . . . The phrase "energy conservation," associated with the oil crunch° of the 1970s, has an unpalatable, age-of-limits° connotation. Yet efficient energy use can actually be the muscular° approach and need not imply deprivation.° There is a big difference between putting on a sweater and switching to a high-efficiency heat pump so the house can be as warm as you like.

    . . . Opportunities . . . exist for substantial energy conservation at the industrial level. Boeing has cut its lighting costs—a significant expense to a company whose manufacturing sites° must be large enough to contain 747s°—by up to 90 percent using conservation techniques. The large process motors that drive factory equipment are the No. 1 consumers of U.S. electrical current: A new generation of these devices requires just half the power of older models. Replacing existing industrial-process motors with the advanced models would, in itself, reduce the country's electricity consumption by about a quarter.

    Early in the next century, cars may have "hybrid" engines that achieve much higher gasoline mileage by combining the features of electric and piston power: Toyota will soon market in Japan the first hybrid, a four-door sedan that gets 66 mpg.° Cars also may run on "fuel cells," clean electrochemical generators that convert a much higher percentage of fuel energy into forward motion than does internal combustion. Ethanol, a petroleum substitute, may soon be manufactured economically from a genetically engineered form of switch grass: Fuel distilled from vegetation is greenhouse friendly because as plants grow they withdraw carbon dioxide from the air.

    . . . The first step in greenhouse policy is for everyone to calm down. Affordable° reforms can sustain global affluence° while moving society beyond dependence on fossil fuels. No doom° awaits us; but there is plenty of work to do, and it's time to get started.

Glosses (right margin):

oppose

decide

sad

probably

shortage / period of restrictions

straightforward
suffering

buildings
huge jet airplanes

miles per gallon

Cost-effective / wealth
bad luck

LEARNING ACTIVITIES

A. Check your comprehension

1. Read each statement below, then decide if it is true or false, depending on the information in the reading.

   a. It is certain that greenhouse gases are causing the Earth to warm.

   b. The chemistry of Earth's atmosphere is changing because of an increase in airborne carbon dioxide (CO_2).

   c. Many American economists want a reduction in greenhouse emissions.

   d. Since 1970 there has been a significant increase in smog caused by automobile emissions in the United States.

   e. Positive solutions to environmental problems usually begin with the criticism of new ideas for change.

   f. Burning fossil fuels releases artificial greenhouse gases into the atmosphere.

   g. Boeing, a company that manufactures 747 jet aircraft, has done little to conserve energy.

   h. Car manufacturers, such as Toyota, are designing more fuel-efficient vehicles.

   i. Automobiles in the 21st century will probably run on mostly fossil fuels.

   j. There is little hope that industry will find solutions to conserve energy in the 21st century.

2. Find the line(s) in the reading where the following statements are expressed in different words.

   a. Studies of global warming have had unclear results.

   b. Negatively speaking, global warming is the result of pure computer simulation.

   c. Whatever your opinion may be, there are chemical changes in the atmosphere.

   d. Soon the air we breathe will have double the CO_2 that it had in the 1800s.

   e. Economists seldom defend the environment since they are interested in economic growth.

   f. An example of environmental policy with poor economic results is the Endangered Species Act.

   g. Great technology comes after everybody is unhappy with a problem.

   h. If you make better use of energy, you need not restrict it.

   i. Nothing uses more energy than motors that drive industrial machinery.

   j. If you don't like electric cars, you can soon buy an electric-gas car.

k. You may soon buy a car run on fuel cells, which are more efficient than the internal combustion engine.

l. It is much better to grow plants for fuel to decrease CO_2 twice.

B. Increasing your word power

The reading selection for this chapter uses many opposites to explain the two sides of global warming. For each expression in the list, find a *negative* counterpart in the article, copy it, and then write a sentence using the new word.

EXAMPLE: example = counterexample

Not every space flight is an incontestable success, but fixing the Hubble telescope is a prominent counterexample.

1. pro	**6.** positive	**11.** incontestable
2. alarmist	**7.** clear	**12.** happiness
3. at best	**8.** natural	**13.** conclusive
4. clear message	**9.** conservation	**14.** plant
5. increased	**10.** affordable	**15.** to exceed

C. Wishful thinking

Complete the following sentences with appropriate verb forms from the list below.

would conserve	would drive	would have	would use
would donate	would enforce	would love	would recycle

1. If people _____ more paper products, we would not have to cut down so many trees.

2. If we would plant more trees, we _____ more clean oxygen to breathe.

3. We would not worry so much about war if people _____ each other more.

4. If rich people _____ more food to the poor, there would be less hunger in the world.

5. If no one _____ illegal drugs, there would be less crime everywhere.

6. Our world would have cleaner water if governments _____ their anti-pollution laws more strictly.

7. There would be less air pollution if people _____ their cars and trucks less often.

8. If industry _____ more energy, our global village would be a better place to live.

D. Save our global village!

1. For each environmental problem in the left-hand column, choose an appropriate solution in the right-hand column. You may add your own solutions as well.

ENVIRONMENTAL PROBLEMS	POSSIBLE SOLUTIONS
a. acid rain	Filter all drinking water.
b. toxic wastes	Use less air conditioning.
c. water pollution	Plant millions of trees.
d. global warming	Recycle natural resources.
e. air pollution	Walk or bicycle more often.
f. forest depletion	Fine the polluting factories.
g. lack of fossil fuels	Protect all plants and animals.
h. animal extinction	?
i. thinning of the ozone	?

2. Read the types of Environmental Problems listed above. Then make a list from 1 to 9 of the most serious environmental problems to our global village, in your opinion: 1 = the most serious, 2 = less serious, etc.

3. Discuss your opinions with a classmate.

E. Oh, for a breath of fresh air!

Give an alternative way of expressing the numerical concepts in the sentences below. Then write a new sentence. You may use expressions from the following list.

$1/4$; $1/3$; $1/2$; CO_2; about 2,550; 100% increase; 50%; almost 25%; 33% increase; 33% decrease; out of approximately 2,500, 8 were prize winners; a /the decade

1. Carbon dioxide in the atmosphere has increased by one third.
2. Carbon dioxide is on its way to doubling soon.
3. More than 2,550 economists said greenhouse gases can be reduced without danger to the economy.
4. The 2,500 economists included eight Nobel prize winners.
5. In 1972, one third of American lakes and rivers were safe.
6. Today, almost two thirds are safe.
7. Since 1970, smog has diminished by nearly a third.
8. The number of cars has almost doubled.
9. Ten years later both pollution and costs are declining.
10. The oil crunch of the 1970s is unpleasant to remember.
11. A new generation of motors requires just half the power of older models.
12. Replacing old motors would reduce energy consumption by about a quarter.

F. Problems around the world

Listed below are ten serious problems in our global village. For each problem, indicate the following:

>one or more countries where it is most serious
>
>one or more causes of the problem
>
>one or more solutions to that problem

EXAMPLE: hunger

>The most serious hunger problem is in India. The hunger in India is caused by lack of money. The United Nations should give more food to India.

PROBLEM	COUNTRY(IES)	CAUSE(S)	SOLUTION(S)
1. Hunger	_____	_____	_____
2. Poverty	_____	_____	_____
3. Civil war	_____	_____	_____
4. Illegal drugs	_____	_____	_____
5. Dictatorship	_____	_____	_____
6. Violent crime	_____	_____	_____
7. Nuclear weapons	_____	_____	_____
8. Racial prejudice	_____	_____	_____
9. Gender inequality	_____	_____	_____
10. HIV/AIDS epidemic	_____	_____	_____

G. I'm doing my share

What do you do to protect our natural environment? What more could you do to protect it?

1. Answer these two questions in a written paragraph.

EXAMPLES:

What do I do now? I take brief showers every morning. I walk to school almost every day. I often ride my bicycle to do chores around town. I donate money to the World Wildlife Fund, which protects endangered animals worldwide.

What more could I do? I could use my car even less. I could use biodegradable products. I could talk to children about how to protect the environment for their future.

2. Exchange your paragraphs with a classmate. Then read what he or she wrote, and write some constructive comments about the paragraphs.

H. Environmental problems

First, read each situation. Then discuss your solutions with a classmate by giving your response to each incomplete sentence. Feel free to add additional comments and opinions to your sentences so that you engage in a discussion about our global environment.

1. Forest depletion in the Amazon jungle, especially in Peru and Brazil, is an enormous problem. Each day more than 50,000 acres of trees are cut down, and some endangered animals and medicinal plants are also destroyed in the process.

   a. If I were the president of Peru/Brazil, I would . . .

   b. If I were the secretary general of the United Nations, I would . . .

   c. If I were a Brazilian citizen, I would . . .

2. In Washington, D.C., many crimes are committed by people using handguns. Each day one hundred people are victims of a violent crime there. There are not sufficient police officers to protect local residents and visitors in that city because of insufficient funds.

   a. If I were the chief of police in Washington, D.C., I would . . .

   b. If I were a resident of that city, I would . . .

   c. If I were a visitor to Washington, D.C., I would . . .

3. Many scientists and missionaries to Central and West Africa have contact with animals, bacteria, and viruses. Some fatal diseases result from these contacts, such as the Ebola virus.

   a. If I were the director of a scientific research center, I would . . .

   b. If I were a Central or West African government official, I would . . .

   c. If I were a missionary, I would . . .

I. Alternative energies

With two or three classmates, research and present to your class at least one other source of energy that would be affordable in your country or area. Describe the old and the new sources of energy, and explain the benefits of the one you propose.

EXAMPLES: Alternative energies: wind, sea waves and tides, hydraulic, geothermal, animal, solar, fuel cells, composite materials

VOCABULARY

Greenhouse Common Sense

Nouns

advocates	agriculture	alarmists	approach
affluence	air	analysis	atmosphere

automotive
benefits
business executives
carbon dioxide
cars
catalytic converter
century
chemistry
climate
climate change
club
combustion
common sense
company
connotation
conservation techniques
consumers
costs
counterexample
country
current
cycle
dependence
deprivation
devices
difference
doom
Earth
economists
efficiencies
effort

electricity consumption
energy
energy conservation
engines
expense
factory equipment
features
fishing
forecasts
form
forward motion
fossil fuels
fuel
fuel cells
fuel energy
gases
gasoline mileage
generation
generators
global warming
green zeal
greenhouse
greenhouse emissions
greenhouse policy
group
growth
heat pump
history
house
hybrid
idea

improvement
industrial revolution
initiatives
innovations
invention
jabber
lakes
lawyers
level
lighting costs
lighting standards
manufacturing sites
models
motors
naysayers
number
oil crunch
opportunities
organization
parties
percentage
petroleum substitute
phase
phrase
piston power
plants
plenty
pollution
pollution control
positions

power
predictions
process motors
prosperity
quarter
realm
reform
rivers
round
science
sedan
sides
smog
smog-control
society
statement
step
subject
sweater
swimming
switch grass
terms
theories
time
unhappiness
use
vegetation
winners
work
years

Adjectives

accused
advanced
affordable
age-of-limits
airborne
ambiguous
American
artificial
big
clean

complex
computer-simulated
distilled
early
economic
efficient
electric
electrical
electrochemical
endless

engineered
enough
environmental
existing
expensive
first
four-door
friendly
general
global

gloomy
high-efficiency
high-yield
higher
human
inconclusive
incontestable
industrial
industrial-process
initiative

institutional
internal
large
likely
mild
muscular
negative
new
next
older

positive	safe	stunning	tired	unpalatable
practical	significant	substantial	uncertain	vast
prominent	sound	sustained		

Verbs

achieve	combine	exist	market	result
affect	condemn	get	move	rule
alter	contain	get started	occur	run
appear	convert	grow	prevent	show
argue	cut	harm	prove	sponsor
associate	decline	have	put on	sustain
await	depend	hear	recognize	switch
begin	diminish	imply	reduce	understand
burn	do	increase	release	use
calm down	drive	join	remain	warm
cause	endorse	make	replace	withdraw
change	exceed	manufacture	require	work
check				

Adverbs

actually	eventually	mainly	recently	soon
almost	genetically	nearly	relatively	today
economically	impossibly	normally	simply	usually
especially				

Proper Nouns

Endangered Species Act	Japan	Nobel Prize	Redefining Progress	Toyota
Ethanol				

Expressions

at best	for all intents and purposes	more often than not	on its way	to have some effect
at worst	in itself	of course	pro and con	

Abbreviations and Symbols

747s	1970s	$1/4$	100%	33%
mpg	CO_2	$1/3$	50%	25%
US	21st century	$1/2$		

14 In Search of ETs[1]

<hr>

[1]*ETs* are extraterrestrials (beings from another planet).

The Center for the Study of Extraterrestrial Intelligence (CSETI) is an interesting organization. The main goals of the center are to establish° a research project to contact extraterrestrial civilizations; to build a peaceful relationship with them; and to teach human beings about this subject in a nonharmful° manner.

form

not damaging

Dr. Steven M. Greer founded CSETI in 1991, and today it has more than 900 members worldwide. He and other investigators often visit specific sites° to interact with extraterrestrial spacecrafts° and their occupants. Dr. Greer calls these human contacts "Close Encounters° of the Fifth Kind."

places / space vehicles

Meetings

My name is Dr. Joseph Burkes, MD.° Recently, Dr. Greer invited me to join a group of five CSETI investigators at a remote site in Mexico. First, we set up camp at the base of an active volcano. Then we set up our camera equipment, radar detector, and sleeping bags in a clearing° on a hillside. From this site, we had a good view of a town in the valley below.

Medical Doctor

open field

As we watched, one unidentified° flying object (UFO) appeared, then possibly two, over the town. The objects were amber-colored° and shaped like globes. It seemed that some kind of intelligence was controlling them. Dr. Greer aimed a powerful light to signal° the object. It appeared to signal back.

not named

yellowish

communicate with

The next day we traveled to a new location where UFOs were a common sight. We set up our equipment in a field near an 18,000-foot (5,905-meter)-high volcano named Popocatepetl. Around 11:45 p.m., Dr. Greer saw a light that was moving near our position. We began signaling it with our lights, and it changed direction directly toward us. As it came nearer, we could see that it was shaped like a triangle. It had a white light at each corner and a red beacon° in the center. It was totally silent, highly maneuverable,° and came toward us in a wide arc. Flying close behind the spacecraft was another smaller craft that

light

able to move around

seemed to be escorting° the larger ship that was at least 300 feet (98.42 meters) wide.

accompanying

The spacecraft descended° to less than 500 feet (164.04 meters), then it turned on many powerful lights. It slowed down considerably while continuing to respond to Dr. Greer's light signals. As we rushed to our camera equipment, things started to go wrong. The craft stopped its descent and its flight behavior changed dramatically.° It slowly started to turn in a wide arc, which allowed us to clearly see its underside.° Even though it aborted° its false landing, the spacecraft continued to answer our light signals.

came down

a lot

bottom / stopped

As all this was happening, we suddenly realized that our cameras were not working. It seemed that someone or something did not want us to record this encounter with any type of photographs.

This exciting and memorable experience confirmed to me that we CSETI investigators are doing the correct thing. I believe that we can better understand UFOs by wanting to contact them. Our organization is young and our results are still in their beginning stages, but the prospects are quite promising.°

hopeful

LEARNING ACTIVITIES

A. Check your comprehension

1. Mark the statement which is *not* a goal of CSETI.

_____ To make visits to sites where UFOs may land.

_____ To make contact with ETs on earth or in space.

_____ To make friends with beings from other planets.

_____ To make preparations to protect humans from ETs.

2. Match the names in the left-hand column with their meaning in the right-hand column.

_____ ET   **a.** Large, active volcano in Mexico

_____ UFO   **b.** Author of this reading selection

_____ CSETI   **c.** Founder and director of the CSETI

_____ Popocatepetl   **d.** Unknown extraterrestrial spaceship

_____ Dr. Joseph Burkes **e.** Research center for ET intelligence

_____ Dr. Steven Greer **f.** Being or creature from another planet

3. Mark each of the following statements as true or false, according to the information in the reading. If a statement is false, say why and correct it to make it true.

1. _____ Dr. Burkes took many photographs of several UFOs.

2. _____ The investigators always saw UFOs traveling alone.

3. _____ Communication with the ETs was by radar and radio.

4. _____ Dr. Greer and his investigators saw UFOs in Mexico.

5. _____ The research team stayed overnight at a small hotel.

6. _____ The spacecraft actually landed near the investigators.

7. _____ One UFO was round and another was triangular in shape.

8. _____ Dr. Burkes seemed discouraged by his field experience.

B. Increasing your word power

Write at least three words associated in meaning to the ones below.

EXAMPLE: respond ⟶ signal, answer, contact, signal back

1. signal
2. fly
3. beacon
4. spacecraft
5. descent
6. camera
7. valley
8. powerful
9. sleeping bags
10. equipment
11. peaceful
12. intelligence

C. Narrating a story

First, find the past tense of the following verbs in the reading. Then complete the story below by using some of the past tense verbs. Afterwards, your teacher may ask you to write a story that happened to you.

to . . . invite, set up camp, abort, can, watch, turn on, seem, aim, appear, signal back, travel, see, begin, change direction, come, have, escort, descend, respond, rush, start, be, go wrong, stop, turn, allow, continue, answer, realize, appear, work, want, confirm

    We were about two hours from London, crossing over the Atlantic on the way to the United States. Suddenly, our plane _____ to shake and the sound of the engines _____. I thought everyone had _____ what happened but the only person who _____ to my scared look _____ my son George. A few seconds later, the plane _____ to turn in a wide arc. It _____ that we were returning to London! We _____ slowly and after several minutes the pilot _____ my fears: we _____ mechanical problems and we _____ flying back to Heathrow Airport. My son _____ the videocamera,

_____ it on, and _____ to record everything. Twenty minutes later, I _____ a smaller craft very close to our right wing. George _____ it with the videocamera's lights and the pilot _____ back with his lights! _____ we be in extreme danger? Over Ireland, we _____ direction once more but I _____ see that the small plane still _____ us on the right. After the pilot _____ the landing once, we finally _____ safely at Heathrow. What _____ wrong? One engine had _____ so the pilots _____ us back to London to avoid any unnecessary risks. Of course, when we finally reached the United States, we were six hours behind schedule!

D. What if?

When people read UFO stories, they sometimes think of what they would do if they saw an actual UFO or an ET. What would you do? Think about this as you complete the sentences below using the following pattern: **if + past tense + would + verb.**

EXAMPLE: If I saw a UFO, I would call a TV station.

1. If I (see, sense, receive signals), I would . . .
2. If we (can, plan to, set up camp), we would . . .
3. If Dr. Greer (invite, set up camp, respond my letter), I would . . .
4. If I (can see, start to see, continue to see) . . . , I . . .
5. If scientists (be sure, have proof, think) that UFOs exist, they . . .
6. I really would . . . , if I . . .
7. I don't think I would . . . , if . . .

E. Are we alone?

Some people say Earth is the only planet where there is intelligent life. Others do not believe that. What do you think? Respond to the two questions below, and to the statements below each answer. Your teacher will tell you whether to do this activity with another classmate, or in writing, or both.

1. Do you believe there is intelligent life on other planets?
   _____ Yes, I do. Discuss your reasons and say . . .
   a. why you believe in ET intelligence.
   b. how long you have believed in ETs.
   c. whether or not ETs have visited Earth, and
   d. if so, where, when and how they have done so.

_____ No, I don't. Discuss your reasons and say . . .

a. why you do not believe in ET intelligence.

b. how long you have held that belief.

c. whether ETs will ever visit Earth, and

d. if so, where, when and how they will visit.

2. Have you seen an unidentified flying object (UFO)?

_____ Yes, I have. Discuss your sighting and say . . .

a. exactly what you saw.

b. where you saw the UFO.

c. the date and time you saw it.

d. what the UFO looked like.

e. how long you saw it.

f. who was with you at the time.

g. how you or others reacted to the UFO.

_____ No, I haven't. Discuss . . .

a. what you would do if you ever saw one.

b. the most likely place you would see a UFO.

c. what the spacecraft might look like.

d. who would be the occupants of the craft.

e. how the occupants would communicate with you.

F. A very close encounter

1. Dr. Greer's research team made some spectacular sightings during their second night in Mexico. Make three simple drawings that show what the team saw.

2. Below each of your three drawings, write a short caption explaining what the drawing shows.

3. Share your drawings and captions with those of a classmate. Discuss them together.

G. A special invitation

Imagine that Dr. Greer has invited you to join him on a CSETI investigation in Egypt.

1. Make a list of ten things that you would take on the trip.

2. Next to each item, explain why you would take it along.

3. Speak with a classmate: Name the ten things on your list, and say why you would take them with you to Egypt.

4. With your classmate, join another pair of students. Compare your lists and discuss your reasons for listing the things you would take with you on your CSETI investigation.

H. Research project

Do a research project on *one* of the following topics. Use an encyclopedia and/or the Internet to find interesting information. First, make notes on your findings. Then use your notes to write two or three paragraphs on the most important information. Your teacher may ask you to present your report to the class.

Mind reading	Crop circles worldwide
Haunted houses	Geometric lines in Nazca, Peru
Remote viewing	Extraterrestrial intelligence (ETI)
Psychic phenomena	Unidentified Flying Objects (UFOs)
Extrasensory perception (ESP)	UFO sightings in Roswell, New Mexico

Maya / Quechua / Egyptian constructions based on astronomical knowledge

VOCABULARY

In Search of ETs

Nouns

arc	detector	intelligence	photographs	sleeping bags
base	direction	investigators	position	spacecraft
beacon	encounter	kind	project	stages
behavior	equipment	landing	prospects	subject
camera	experience	light	radar	town
camp	field	location	relationship	triangle
center	flight	manner	research	type
civilizations	globes	members	results	UFO
clearing	goals	meters	ship	underside
contacts	group	object	sight	valley
corner	hillside	occupants	signals	view
craft	human beings	organization	sites	volcano
descent				

Adjectives

active	exciting	larger	powerful	smaller
amber-colored	extraterrestrial	main	promising	specific
beginning	false	maneuverable	red	unidentified
close	flying	memorable	remote	white
common	human	nonharmful	shaped	wide
correct	interesting	peaceful	silent	young

Verbs

abort	change	fly	realize	start
aim	confirm	found	record	stop
allow	contact	go wrong	respond	teach
answer	continue	happen	rush	travel
appear	control	interact	seem	turn on
begin	descend	invite	set up	understand
believe	escort	join	signal	visit
build	establish	move	slow down	watch

Adverbs

below	directly	often	recently	totally
clearly	dramatically	possibly	slowly	worldwide
considerably	highly	quite	suddenly	

Proper Nouns

CSETI	Dr. Steven M. Greer	Mexico	Popocatepetl

Expressions

close behind	in search of

Abbreviations

Dr.	ET	MD	p.m.	UFOs

Vocabulary Review
Unit VII

A. Word sets

In each word set below, cross out the word that does *not* belong to it. Then explain why you crossed out the word in each set.

EXAMPLE: sedan / ship / ~~site~~ / car
The noun *site* does not refer to a type of motorized vehicle.

1. doom / gloomy / winner / smog   _____
2. object / valley / hillside / volcano   _____
3. to drive / to fly / to travel / to seem   _____
4. beacon / vegetation / radar / signal   _____
5. white / distilled / red / amber-colored   _____
6. generator / engine / combustion / beacon   _____
7. encounters / lawyers / naysayers / investigators _____
8. prosperity / clearing / affluence / economist _____

B. Reading for meaning

Read the selection below. Then complete the reading with appropriate words and phrases from the following list.

ET, extraterrestrial, hillside, suddenly, light, directly, craft, doom, beacon, center, spacecraft, powerful, Air pollution, society, realize, fossil fuels, remote, industrial, global warming, watching

A Close Encounter

I had just gone to bed when I felt a strange sensation in my body. I got up and looked out the bedroom window of my small house which stands atop a _____ on a _____ island in Washington State. _____, I saw a triangular spacecraft _____ over the large field out front. The _____ made no sound and it did not move.

I continued _____ as a powerful white _____ radiated downward from the _____ of the spaceship. A human-looking form appeared in the bright _____. I was terrified.

"Do not be afraid. I mean no harm to you," said the _____ creature who seemed to be speaking within my own mind. "I have come to warn

you. Your planet is in danger of total destruction. Your _____
_____ are nearly gone. _____ wastes are everywhere.
_____ _____ is killing your people worldwide. And
_____ will be your final doom."

    When I heard the word "_____," I woke up with a cold sweat all
over my body. "My gosh," I thought, "I was dreaming." The _____ and
the _____ were not real, but the message of the strange visitor seemed
_____. When will our _____ wake up from its reality and be-
gin to _____ the fate of our global village?

C. Which do you prefer?

Mark or write in the blank *one* preference to complete each sentence below. Then read
aloud your preferences to a classmate.

   1. I wish there would be . . .
   _____ less air   _____ more nonharmful _____
   pollution   products

   2. I don't like wasting . . .
   _____ fossil fuels   _____ electricity   _____

   3. More often than not I . . .
   _____ conserve energy   _____ prevent waste   _____

   4. Our Earth's future seems . . .
   _____ promising   _____ uncertain   _____

   5. In my country, energy conservation is . . .
   _____ quite low   _____ quite high   _____

   6. I definitely . . .
   _____ believe in ET   _____ do not believe   _____
              intelligence   in UFOs

   7. In the future I hope to . . .
   ___ see a UFO   _____ travel to another _____
                                           planet

   8. If I would see a UFO, I would . . .
   _____ call the   _____ phone a friend   _____
   police

   9. I'd like to travel in a . . .
   _____ UFO   _____ supersonic   _____
                                           aircraft

   10. I believe that someday I will visit . . .
   _____ the moon   _____ the planet   _____
                                           Mars

D. Getting to know you

Ask a classmate the questions below. Write down his or her answers. When you finish, your classmate should ask *you* the questions. Your teacher may ask you to explain why you chose certain preferences.

1. Do you know what fossil fuels are? If so, name one or two fossil fuels. How long do you think they will last on our Earth? If you don't know what fossil fuels are, what do you think they might be?

2. Do you believe that the Earth's climate is changing? If so, what do you think is causing that change? Is the change good or bad? Do you think that the Earth's climate will change dramatically in the next ten years? Why?

3. What are you doing to protect the Earth's environment for future generations? What more could you do?

4. Do you believe that extraterrestrial beings exist? If so, will they help us learn to protect our global village? Do you think that human beings will destroy the Earth someday? Please explain your answer.

5. I will say some adjectives. Tell me if the adjectives describe you. Say "Yes," "No," or "It depends" (and explain on what it depends).

tired	complex	ambiguous	practical
gloomy	friendly	muscular	prominent
peaceful			

E. Looking toward the future

Complete the crossword puzzle on the next page.

Looking toward the future

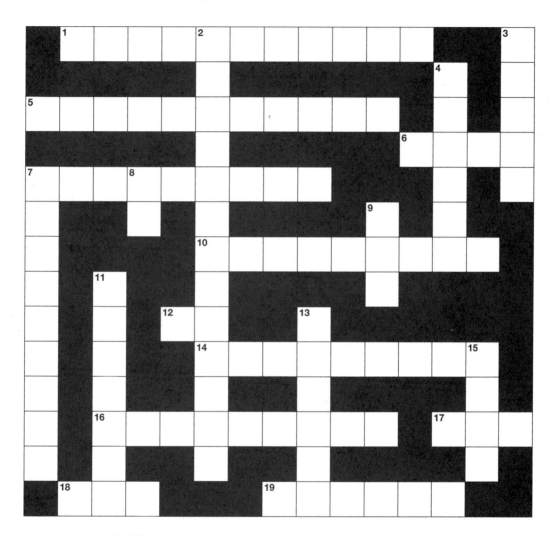

ACROSS

1. Suffering
5. Space vehicles
6. The opposite of "dangerous"
7. Important
10. Fumes, gases
12. The abbreviation for "extraterrestrial"
14. Not clear, vague
16. Wealth
17. Pro and _____
18. The opposite of "used"
19. Much, in abundance

DOWN

2. Certain, without question
3. Places
4. Light
7. Hopeful
8. The abbreviation for "medical doctor"
9. Another word for "large"
11. Weather conditions
13. To communicate with someone
15. A mixture of smoke and fog

Answer Key

Answer Key

This key contains the answers only to those activities in which there are preestablished responses. Optional answers appear in parentheses.

Chapter 1
Swim First, Walk Later

A. **1.** B, B, B, A, C

2. 5, 1, 3, 2, 6, 4

B. **3.** "water babies," water filter, water ski, water polo

4. **a.** Romanian **b.** Japanese **c.** Czech **d.** Chilean **e.** Yugoslav **f.** American **g.** Canadian **h.** Russian **i.** Chinese

5. wonderful, gently, cheerfully, instructor, infant, enjoy, surface, exhale

a. wonderful (great), terrible, great (wonderful)

b. softly (gently), gently (softly), roughly

c. happily (cheerfully), cheerfully (happily), sadly

d. teacher (instructor), student, teacher (instructor)

e. Adults, babies (infants), infants (babies)

f. like (enjoy), enjoy (like), dislike

g. bottom, surface (top), top (surface)

h. exhale (breathe out), inhale, exhale (breathe out)

C. **1.** a, a, Some, a, a, an, some

2. the, the, a, the, a, the, A, the

D. watches, goes, has, sleeps, watches, has, is, feeds, plays, takes, comes, tries, goes, is

E. **1.** worked—to work; began—to begin; noticed—to notice; dove—to dive; swam—to swim; floated—to float; had—to have; taught—to teach; learned—to learn; became—to become

2. had, was, taught, floated, swam, became, had

F.   **1.** better **2.** healthier **3.** more **4.** more **5.** more **6.** better

Chapter 2
An Orphanage for Some Big Babies

A.   **1.** a **2.** b **3.** c **4.** d **5.** c **6.** c

B.   **1. a.** robust **b.** grief **c.** protects **d.** trained, save
       2. a. poachers, grief, trinkets, banned
          b. donations, coworkers, releases
          c. companions, Gradually, mischievous

Vocabulary Review
Unit I

A.   **1.** *Nairobi* is a city, not a country.
       2. *Minds* refers to an abstract idea, rather than to a specific part of the human body.
       3. *Crops* refers to things, not to people.
       4. *Stressed* is a negative health condition.
       5. *To drive* does not refer to a sport.
       6. A *youngster* is not a kind of profession.
       7. *Trinket* refers to a thing, not to a place.

B. *Paragraph 1:* village, sisters, healthy, swimming, elephant, youngster, mischievous
     Paragraph 2: mornings, walks, jogs, dives, begins, cheerfully, rubdown, water baby, to thrive, gives
     Paragraph 3: protect, game warden, confident, poachers, trinkets, ivory, slogan

E.   **Children and animals**

Chapter 3
Finding Yourself on Your Family Tree

A.   **1.** false **2.** false **3.** true **4.** true **5.** false

B.   **1.** grandparents **2.** son **3.** daughters, granddaughters **4.** Jones **5.** cousins
6. sisters-in-law **7.** Cary Bedford

D.

E.   **1. a.** period / documents (written materials) **b.** unique / negative conditions
c. repeat / relate to comprehension **d.** weak / positive ideas **e.** change /
documents (written materials) **f.** experience / people **g.** marriage / school
subjects (classes)

   2. a. history **b.** scrapbook **c.** unique **d.** experience **e.** diary **f.** important **g.** repeat

Chapter 4
The Food of Love

A.   **1. a.** Palermo **b.** soccer **c.** to get some tickets **d.** dancing **e.** a song from
long ago

B.   **1. a.** quiet, silent **b.** puffing, tired **c.** open door, cracked open **d.** soccer,
tickets **e.** take, find **f.** music, in each other's arms **g.** enter, head out
h. oldies, love **i.** soccer, stadium **j.** Swiss chard, green stuff **k.** washing
dishes, cleaning **l.** went, ran

C. *Paragraph 1:* was, sprang, were, could, got, bolted, said
Paragraph 2: arrived, realized, was, left, ran, could, entered, heard, didn't, made, grabbed
Paragraph 3: left, could, noticed, was, wanted, pushed, peeked, was, was
Paragraph 4: left, began

Vocabulary Review
Unit II

A.   1. *Pattern* is not related to music.

2. *Effort* is not related to sports.

3. *Palermo* is a city, not a person's first name.

4. *Quickly* does not carry the feeling of carefulness.

5. *Lunch* is not related to obtaining information.

6. *Side* is not related to food.

B. *Paragraph 1:* study, history, find out, relatives, parents, generations
Paragraph 2: curiosity, romantic, affairs, pasta, child, marriage
Paragraph 3: letters, scrapbooks, members, takes, afternoon, fascinating, powerful

E. All in the family

Chapter 5
The King and I

A.   1. **a.** relax **b.** men **c.** like **d.** helped **e.** spoke **f.** like **g.** kind

2. PEOPLE

a. King Taufa'ahau Tupou IV **b.** Jesus Christ **c.** Edwin **d.** Jim Hendrickson

PLACES

a. Good Samaritan Inn **b.** South Pacific Ocean **c.** United States **d.** *fale* (at the Good Samaritan Inn) **e.** gym (gymnasium) **f.** Royal Palace office

B.   **1.** rode **2.** took **3.** shook **4.** thought **5.** spent **6.** met **7.** left **8.** knelt
         9. knew **10.** wore

Chapter 6
Surprising Reykjavík

A.   **2. a.** cool **b.** low **c.** few **d.** low **e.** high **f.** many **g.** some

B.   **1. a.** people and animals **b.** people and animals **c.** people and animals
         d. people and animals **e.** people **f.** people and animals **g.** people
         h. people **i.** people and animals **j.** people

    2. a. A *horde* is not a place to live.

      b. *Whales* are not formed by water.

      c. A *nation* is not round in shape.

      d. *Females* are not an animal type.

      e. *Recreation* is not a specific pastime.

      f. *Species* do not refer to water.

      g. *Lava fields* are not formed by water.

    3. a. driving **b.** skating **c.** hunting **d.** snowboarding **e.** skateboarding
         f. biking **g.** whale watching **h.** taking pictures **i.** job hunting **j.** swimming **k.** sea kayaking **l.** ice fishing

Vocabulary Review
Unit III

A.   **1.** *Seabirds* do not live permanently in water.

    2. *Rare* does not refer to size.

    3. *Reykjavík* is a city, not a country.

    4. *At home* does not refer to a time period.

    5. *To whisper* does not refer to traveling.

    6. *To show up* does not refer to photography.

    7. *Publishing* is a business, not a sport.

B. *Paragraph 1:* young, began, fascinating, dressed, sneakers, camera
      Paragraph 2: United States, friendly, trucks, smile, shook, sunny
      Paragraph 3: outdoors, stayed, night, surprise, like, love

E. Around the world

Chapter 7
A Language Lesson I Learned

A.   **1.** funny **2.** easy **3.** important **4.** quite important **5.** are not **6.** Watching TV in the foreign language **7.** I took **8.** Rome, Italian **9.** comedian, Italian, slang **10.** dream

B.   **2. a.** expatriates **b.** megastars, megastar / megastar **c.** Monolinguals, polyglots **d.** [open answer] **e.** unacceptable/useless, useful / relevant

C.   *Paragraph 1:* At times, Mind you, to this day
Paragraph 2: to get my point across, Granted, Excuse me
Paragraph 3: to no avail, to go to waste
Paragraph 4: Back home, Thanks to, to get a laugh, in the end
Paragraph 5: to rattle on, I was struck dumb, fell for
Paragraph 6: in no time, Good luck

D.

CITY	COUNTRY	CONTINENT	LANGUAGE
Atlanta	United States	North America	English
Buenos Aires	Argentina	South America	Spanish
Istanbul	Turkey	Asia	Turkish
Johannesburg	South Africa	Africa	Afrikaans/English
Karachi	Pakistan	Asia	Pakistani
Moscow	Russia	Europe	Russian
New Delhi	India	Asia	Hindi
Osaka	Japan	Asia	Japanese
Québec	Canada	North America	French
Rome	Italy	Europe	Italian
Sydney	Australia	Australia	English
Tel Aviv	Israel	Middle East	Hebrew

Chapter 8
Hooked on Telenovelas

A.   **1.** d **2.** g **3.** h **4.** b **5.** a **6.** e **7.** c **8.** f

   1. 125 countries

   2. Mexico, Yugoslavia, Serbia, Croatia, China, Indonesia, Philippines, Australia

   3. **a.** *Simplemente María* **b.** *Dallas* and *Dynasty* **c.** *Los Ricos También Lloran* ("The Rich Cry Too"), *Thalia, Cuna de Lobos* ("Den of Wolves")

   4. The soap operas best represent the American dream.

B.   **1.** c, a, d, f, g, e, b, h

   2. **a.** to air a telenovela, to act in a movie, to star in a movie

      b. to be mobbed by people, to dip in ratings, to give up one's child, to tear oneself apart

      c. to be at a premium, to become famous, to fall in love

C. *Paragraph 1:* Once upon a time, In those days, at a premium, In time, fell in love, for a moment, hooked on, Nevertheless, give up
   Paragraph 2: One day, in time, modus vivendi
   Paragraph 3: By chance, fell in love, fall in love
   Paragraph 4: One day, swept María off her feet, happily ever after

F.   **1.** action **2.** cartoon **3.** mystery **4.** comedy **5.** drama **6.** Western **7.** science fiction

Vocabulary Review
Unit IV

A.   **1.** *Den* is not a type of food.

   2. *Accent* does not refer to people.

   3. *Decent* has a positive meaning, not a negative one.

   4. *Venetian* does not refer to a nationality.

   5. *Ethnic* does not refer to something worldwide.

   6. *Mariana* is a person's name, not a country.

   7. An *expatriate* is not a profession.

   8. An *enterprise* is not a kind of store.

B. *Paragraph 1:* television, remember, screen, enormous
   Paragraph 2: pals, classic, megastars, hooked, hard-core, watch, cinema, dream
   Paragraph 3: grandparents, at times, scorn, high-tech, outside, rattle, going to waste, become
   Paragraph 4: still, prime time, given up

E. Home entertainment

Chapter 9
Cloning: Duplicating Human Beings

A.   **1.** False **2.** False **3.** True **4.** False **5.** True **6.** False **7.** True **8.** False **9.** True **10.** False

C.   **1.** clone, cloned; destroy; inform, information; accept, donation (donor), donated; growth; know

2. clone, donate, accept, reproduction, know, knowledge (information), know, growth, destructive

D. copy, cloning, cloned, replaced, egg, uterus, Dolly

E.

F.   **1. a.** Can, can **b.** Can, can't **c.** Can, can **d.** Can, can't **e.** could, could, couldn't

2. a. cannot (can't) **b.** can **c.** couldn't **d.** can **e.** can, cannot (can't) **f.** can, couldn't

Chapter 10
Extending the Human Life Span

A.   **1.** Ms. Jeanne Calment was 122 years old, probably the world's oldest person.

2. China (how free radicals protect human tissue, and how traditional Chinese medicines slow the aging process); England (the role of the telemere in the aging process); United States (how eating fewer calories can slow the aging process); Australia (how health problems affect advanced age).

3. Dr. Manton believes that many factors affect the human life span.

4. There will be no maximum age limit in the future.

5. World—65 years; Japan—80 years; Africa—50 years; Sierra Leone—40 years; developing countries—75 years; least developed countries—52 years

B. *Paragraph 1:* upper
Paragraph 2: older / younger; older / younger / healthier / weaker
Paragraph 3: older / younger; healthier / weaker / younger / older
Paragraph 4: older / younger; higher / lower
Paragraph 5: major

Vocabulary Review
Unit V

A.   1. *Sperm* refers to males.

       2. *Hong Kong* is a city, not a continent.

       3. *Process* does not refer to copying.

       4. *Calories* does not refer to genetics.

       5. *Leader* is not a specific profession.

       6. *North Carolina* is a state, not a country.

       7. *To isolate* does not refer to growing or multiplying.

       8. *To fertilize* does not refer to searching for something.

B. *Paragraph 1:* healthy, centuries, exciting, Immortality, affect
Paragraph 2: human beings, probably, numbers, grow, medical doctors, health, major, chronic, expect, technology, leaders, methods, reproduction, nearly
Paragraph 3: All around the world, especially, Therefore, survive, In short, argue
Paragraph 4: dramatic, protect, difference, human

E. Human life sciences

Chapter 11
Mini Computer Moguls

A.   **1.** 16, Minneapolis; Danny Kalmick, Kalmick & Co. Computing, California; 18, Orlando; 17, Pixelstorm Inc., Orlando, Florida

    2. a. young computer entrepreneurs **b.** he was too young for the job **c.** successful **d.** work in the United States

E.   **1.** is planning; am planning **2.** is running; is thriving **3.** are . . . fixing / operating / custom-building; operating/fixing/troubleshooting **4.** are doing; are using **5.** are becoming; are offering **6.** are . . . custom-building / planning / operating / fixing; are . . . troubleshooting

Chapter 12
Tower Power

A.   **1.** g **2.** b **3.** f **4.** h **5.** e **6.** c **7.** i **8.** d **9.** a

    1. Hong Kong **2.** 1,509 **3.** Petronas Towers **4.** 1974 **5.** New York **6.** New York **7.** Chrysler Building **8.** 1913 **9.** 1909 **10.** Singer Building

    1. The title "Tower Power" represents a competition for building the tallest skyscrapers. (The competition parallels the expanding business of corporations.)

    3. Nina Wang. She lives in Hong Kong. She wants to build the tallest building in the world.

C.   **a.** drawing board **b.** office buildings **c.** world leader **d.** power house **e.** steel-beam **f.** skyscraper **g.** high-rise crown **h.** Nina Tower **i.** business district **j.** Empire State Building

Hyphenated adjectives

    1. high-cost **2.** high-rise **3.** high-speed **4.** mass-produced **5.** steel-beam

Word families

    1. architect; to finance, financial; globe; to personalize, personable; residential; to plan; admirer; construction, constructor; corporation

    2. architectural, admirable, high-rise, financial, steel, Admirers, corporate, planned

Vocabulary Review
Unit VI

A.   **1.** *Power* does not refer to money directly.

    2. A *neighbor* is not a machine.

    3. A *detail* does not refer to living in a community.

4. *Chicago* is a city in the United States, not in Asia.

5. An *entrepreneur* is a person, not an enterprise.

6. A *license* does not refer to a type of building.

7. The verb *to reach* does not refer to shining outward.

8. The adjective *universal* does not refer to something wonderful.

9. The noun *patterns* does not refer to business.

B. *Paragraph 1:* work, professional
Paragraph 2: corporate job, headquarters, president, company, advice
Paragraph 3: business district, skyscraper, powerful, marketplace, high-speed, crucial, clients
Paragraph 4: architect, homes, At present, residential, earn, challenges, personal

E. Business affairs

Chapter 13
Greenhouse Common Sense

A.   **1. a.** False **b.** True **c.** True **d.** False **e.** True **f.** True **g.** False **h.** True
i. False **j.** False

  2. a. "The science of global warming is ambiguous."

    b. " . . . at worst, it's a realm of computer-simulated jabber . . . "

    c. " . . . it is incontestable that the chemistry of the atmosphere is changing."

    d. " . . . carbon dioxide has increased . . . and appears on its way to doubling."

    e. " . . . economists—a group not normally accused of green zeal . . . "

    f. " . . . Of course, not every reform works well in economic terms, the Endangered Species Act being a prominent counterexample."

    g. "Next comes a phase of general unhappiness in which lawyers rule. Then innovations occur—such as the invention of the catalytic converter . . . "

    h. "Yet efficient energy use can actually be the muscular approach and need not imply deprivation."

    i. "The large process motors that drive factory equipment are the No. 1 consumers of U.S. electrical current."

    j. " . . . cars may have "hybrid" engines . . . by combining the features of electric and piston power . . . "

    k. "Cars also may run on "fuel cells," clean electrochemical generators that convert a much higher percentage of fuel energy into forward motion than does internal combustion."

    l. "Fuel distilled from vegetation is greenhouse friendly because as plants grow they withdraw carbon dioxide from the air."

B. **1.** con **2.** naysayer **3.** at worst **4.** jabber **5.** decreased (reduced, diminished) **6.** negative **7.** ambiguous **8.** artificial **9.** consumption **10.** impossibly expensive **11.** uncertain **12.** unhappiness **13.** inconclusive **14.** fossil **15.** to cut (to reduce, to decrease)

C. **1.** would recycle **2.** would have **3.** would love **4.** would donate **5.** would use **6.** would enforce **7.** would drive **8.** would conserve

E. **1.** (33%) **2.** 100% increase **3.** about 2,550 **4.** 8 **5.** 33% ($1/3$) **6.** $2/3$ (66%) **7.** 33% ($1/3$) decrease **8.** 100% increase **9.** a decade **10.** the decade of 1970–1979 **11.** $1/2$ (50%) **12.** $1/4$ (25%)

Chapter 14
In Search of ETs

A. **1.** To make preparations to protect humans from ETs.

    2. f, d, e, a, b, c

    3. False, False, False, True, False, False, True, False

B. **1.** answer, respond, contact **2.** flight, descend, arc, maneuverable **3.** lights, turn on, aim **4.** UFO, fly, descend **5.** slowly, fly, descend **6.** set up, aim, photograph **7.** field, hillside, clearing, volcano **8.** lights, silent, maneuverable, extraterrestrial **9.** field, clearing, set up camp **10.** sleeping bags, cameras, lights, set up, craft, ship, radar **11.** silent, memorable, nonharmful **12.** human beings, extraterrestrials, signals, investigators, civilization

C. seemed, changed, realized, responded, was, started, appeared, descended, confirmed, had, were, set up, turned, started, saw, signalled, answered, Could, changed, could, escorted, aborted, landed, went, stopped, rushed

D. **1.** I saw / sensed / received **2.** we could / planned to / set up camp **3.** Dr. Greer invited / set up camp / responded **4.** I could see / started to see / continued to see **5.** scientists were sure / had proof / thought

Vocabulary Review
Unit VII

A. 1. *Winner* has a positive meaning.
2. *Object* does not refer to a natural feature.
3. *To seem* does not refer to movement.
4. *Vegetation* is not used for communicating with people.
5. *Distilled* is not a color.
6. *Beacon* does not refer to mechanized power.
7. *Encounters* does not refer to human beings.
8. *Clearing* does not refer to money.

B. *Paragraph 1:* hillside, remote, Suddenly, directly, craft
Paragraph 2: watching, beacon, center, light
Paragraph 3: extraterrestrial, fossil fuels, Industrial, Air pollution, global warming
Paragraph 4: doom, spacecraft, ET, powerful, society, realize

E. Looking toward the future

Copyrights and Acknowledgments

For permission to use the adapted and extracted selections reprinted in this book, the authors are grateful to the following publishers and copyright holders:

CLONING: DUPLICATING HUMAN BEINGS Adapted from "Cloning: Duplicating Humans," The Plain Truth. Copyright © 1977 Ambassador College. All rights reserved.

EXTENDING THE HUMAN LIFE SPAN Reprinted with permission from "Extending the Human Life Span," by Mark Rowh, *The Rotarian*, January 1998.

FINDING YOURSELF ON YOUR FAMILY TREE Copyright Mary Augusta Rogers / Originally published in *Woman's Day* Magazine 1977.

THE FOOD OF LOVE Reprinted from *U.S. Airways Attaché Magazine* with permission of Pace Communications © 1997.

GREENHOUSE COMMON SENSE Copyright December 1, 1997, *U.S. News and World Report*.

HOOKED ON TELENOVELAS Reprinted courtesy of *Hemispheres*, the magazine of United Airlines 1997, © Sam Quiñones.

IN SEARCH OF ETs Permission granted by Dr. Joseph Burkes, MD.

THE KING AND I Permission granted by James M. Hendrickson.

A LANGUAGE LESSON I LEARNED Reprinted by permission from *Outside* magazine Copyright © 1997, Mariah Publications Corporation.

MINI COMPUTER MOGULS Copyright, 1997, *U.S. News and World Report*.

AN ORPHANAGE FOR SOME BIG BABIES Reprinted by permission of *Smithsonian*. From *Smithsonian* (March 1997).

SURPRISING REYKJAVIK Reprinted by permission from *Outside* magazine Copyright © 1997, Mariah Publications Corporation.

SWIM FIRST, WALK LATER Adapted with permission from "Pool and Cradle," by Nina Kryukova, *Soviet Life*, December 1979.

TOWER POWER Reprinted with permission from "Tower Power," by Charles Lockwood, *Hemispheres* Magazine, September 1997.

Photo Credits

p. 2: E. Sander/Gamma-Liaison; p. 12: Sneesby & Wilkins/Tony Stone Images; p. 26: © Bachmann/The Image Works; p. 36: J. L. Bulcao/Gamma-Liaison; p. 50: Photo supplied courtesy of Jim Hendrickson; p. 51: Photo supplied courtesy of Jim Hendrickson; p. 52: Photo supplied courtesy of Jim Hendrickson; p. 60: Jean Pragen/Tony Stone Images; p. 74: Lawrence Migdale/Stock Boston; p. 84: Bob Daemmrich/Stock Boston; p. 100: Elizabeth Crews/Stock Boston; p. 110: Gilles Fonlupt/Gamma; p. 124: Eric Sander/Gamma-Liaison; p. 134: John Mead/Science Photo Library/Photo Researchers Inc.; p. 150: Bruce Forster/Tony Stone Images; p. 160: Joe McBride/Tony Stone Images